# DANISH YEARBOOK
# OF
# PHILOSOPHY

VOLUME 37

# DANISH YEARBOOK OF PHILOSOPHY

VOLUME 37

2002

MUSEUM TUSCULANUM PRESS
UNIVERSITY OF COPENHAGEN 2003

Published for
Dansk Filosofisk Selskab
in cooperation with
the Philosophical Societies of Aarhus and Odense
and with financial support from
the Danish Research Council for the Humanities

*

EDITORIAL BOARD:

FINN COLLIN
University of Copenhagen
Chairman

UFFE JUUL JENSEN
University of Aarhus

SVEN ERIK NORDENBO
University of Copenhagen

STIG ANDUR PEDERSEN
Roskilde University Centre

ERICH KLAWONN
Odense University

HANS SIGGAARD JENSEN
Copenhagen Business School

MOGENS PAHUUS
Aalborg University

*

Articles for consideration and all editorial communications should be sent in three copies to:
Danish Yearbook of Philosophy
University of Copenhagen, Department of Philosophy
Njalsgade 80, DK 2300 Copenhagen S, Denmark

Business communications, including subscriptions and orders for reprints, should
be addressed to the publishers:
MUSEUM TUSCULANUM PRESS
Njalsgade 92
DK 2300 Copenhagen S
Denmark

*

© 2003 DANISH YEARBOOK OF PHILOSOPHY
COPENHAGEN, DENMARK
PRINTED IN DENMARK
BY SPECIAL-TRYKKERIET VIBORG

ISBN 87-7289-863-1
ISSN 0070-2749

## CONTENTS

Kasper Lippert-Rasmussen: *Must Morality Motivate?* ............................... 7

Lars Gundersen: *Necessity, Identity and Time* ............................................ 37

Morten Ebbe Juul Nielsen: *Liberalism, Neutrality, and Civil Society* ....... 57

Stig Rasmussen: *The Very Idea of a Benchmark of Truth* ......................... 75

Tomáš Marvan: *On Brandomian Aporia (And One Way Out)* ................... 93

Peter Wolsing: *Is Reason Communicative? Some Critical Remarks on Habermas* .................................................................................................... 103

# MUST MORALITY MOTIVATE?

KASPER LIPPERT-RASMUSSEN

University of Copenhagen

Abstract

Internalism – here the view that moral judgments entail motivation – is often taken to support non-cognitivism about morality. However, Michael Smith has defended a variety of it in combination with a cognitivist account of morality. Despite the eminence of Smith's contribution, his case in favour of internalism is flawed. I distinguish several internalist positions and argue that Smith's version, unlike standard ones, expresses a view about, not the nature of the state one is in when one makes a moral judgment, but the norms of practical rationality. I then defend the externalist appeal to the possibility of amoralism. Such an appeal need not beg the question against internalism and can in any case be backed up by independent considerations. Moreover, neither of Smith's two main arguments in favour of internalism – the reliable connection argument and the appeal to rationalism about moral requirements – are sound. Having shored up the case for externalism and dismissed Smith's case against it, I end the essay with a suggestion as to why many philosophers have been attracted to internalism even though the theory turns out to be ill-founded.

## I. Introduction[1]

Most moral theorists believe that there is an intimate connection of some sort between moral judgments and motivation.[2] Whereas externalists claim that these phenomena are contingently, but reliably, correlated, internalists hold the connection to be necessary.[3] For that reason internalism is often seen as offering strong support for non-cognitivism about morality.[4] For given the plausible assumptions that motivation requires desires as well as beliefs and that no beliefs are necessarily connected with desires, it seems to follow that a necessary relation between moral judgments and motivation can obtain only if moral judgments express desires. However, in a number of deservedly influential recent works Michael Smith has defended a particular form of internalism as part of a cognitivist account of morality.[5] In this paper, I argue that, despite the eminence of Smith's contribution, his case in favour of internalism is flawed. First, I distinguish between a number of different internalist positions and explain how Smith's version fits into the landscape. Then, in Sections Three and Four, I discuss the externalist appeal to the possibility of amoralism and Smith's dismissal of this appeal. In Section Five, I turn to the first of Smith's two main arguments in favour of internalism, the reliable connection argument. In Section Six, I consider whether internalism can be defended on the basis of rationalism about moral requirements. Having dismissed Smith's case in favour of internalism, I briefly suggest in the final section why many philosophers have been attracted to internalism even though the theory turns out to be ill-founded.

## II. Forms of internalism

What we might call *generic internalism about moral judgments* can be stated as follows:

> 1. Necessarily, if a person judges that it is morally right that she $\phi$-ies, that person is motivated to $\phi$.

Strictly speaking, (1) is narrower than *generic* internalism about all moral judgments. First, not all moral judgments are self-addressed moral judgments that apply to one's present or future conduct. Some apply to others and some apply to the past. Second, moral judgments need not involve the concept of moral rightness. Instead they might involve concepts such as moral wrongness, justice, generosity, and kindness. For sake of simplicity, however, I shall largely ignore these two finer points.

Internalists need to explain why the conditional in (1) is necessarily true. They agree that it expresses a conceptual truth, but there are different possibilities as to which concept is relevant here. The relevant concept might be that of morality. Alternatively, it might be the more specific concept of moral rightness. If it were the latter, the question whether internalism about moral judgments as such is true – e.g. whether moral judgments involving thick moral concepts such as injustice or unkindness must involve motivation – would remain outstanding. Thirdly, internalists might think that the relevant concept is the concept of judging that something is morally right. If that were so, internalism would not be true in virtue of the content of the concept of morality.[6]

Internalists also need to say whether the motivation to φ and the judgment that it is morally right to φ must be simultaneous.[7] The possibility of delayed motivation appears to undermine internalism. For if moral motivation can obtain after the judgment with which it is associated, there seems to be no basis for denying that I can judge that it is morally right to φ and then – before, as it were, the relevant motivation kicks in – change my mind. In these circumstances I would not have been motivated to φ by my original judgement in which case generic internalism is false. Moreover, even setting aside moral judgments about the past, a requirement of simultaneous motivation would seem implausibly strong. Suppose I judge that it is morally right for me to φ ten years from now. Suppose, moreover, that I am convinced that I can do nothing now to make it more likely that I shall φ at the relevant time and, thus, is in no way motivated now by my judgment.[8] In these circumstances it seems implausible to claim that I have not made a moral judgment since I am not motivated now.

It will be useful at this point to say a word about the internalist's opponent, the externalist. Externalism is often defined as the negation of internalism, but for many purposes this approach is unhelpful.[9] It is clear, for example, that the approach would categorise the perverse view that, necessarily, if a person judges that it is morally right to φ, then that person is motivated *not* to φ as externalist. Fortunately, for present purposes we need not provide a precise definition of externalism. We can simply note, in view of the problem just mentioned, that externalism involves more than the denial of internalism: it involves the claim that there are no interesting necessary connections between moral judgments and motivation.[10]

Note that (1) is weaker than *generic strong internalism about moral judgments*:

(1a) Necessarily, if a person judges that it is morally right that she φ-ies, that person will φ.

(1a) is stronger than (1). If you intentionally perform some act, then you are motivated to perform that act; but there are many acts that one is motivated to perform but fails to perform as a result of stronger and opposing motivations. Almost all internalists find (1a) too strong.[11] In their view, (1a) seems open to obvious counterexamples like those involving depressed or apathetic characters.[12]

Another form of internalism which is stronger than (1) is:

(1b) Necessarily, if a person judges that it is morally right that she φ-ies, that person will be motivated *by that very judgment* to φ.

(1b) says that moral judgments motivate not only necessarily but *intrinsically*: motivation is, as Robert Audi puts it, constitutively internal and not consequentially internal to moral judgments.[13] To see the difference between (1) and (1b) consider the view that in order to make a moral judgment it is conceptually necessary to be in a certain conative state, a state which is distinct from the moral judgment itself and which by itself motivates. A good example here might be a crude, subjective naturalism according to which, first, the belief that some act is morally right is the belief that one approves of it and, second, one necessarily knows, when one approves of an act, that one approves of it. Such naturalists would presumably hold that moral judgment necessarily involves motivation even though on their view it is not the content of the moral judgment but rather the state of approving that motivates. They would endorse internalism while eschewing the idea that moral judgments are intrinsically motivating.

Some considerations adduced in favour of internalism appear to be neutral between (1) and (1b). For instance, Hare's defence of internalism, which appeals to linguistic intuitions concerning the connection between sincere use of words like "ought" and action, seems to be neutral with respect to the source of motivation.

Various forms of internalism that are in one way or another weaker than (1) are also available. One way to weaken (1) is to broaden the internalist's conception of what one is motivated to do by moral judgment. For example:

(1c) Necessarily, if a person judges that it is morally right that she φ-ies, that person will either φ or be otherwise motivated.

"Otherwise motivated" includes ways of acting or feeling that are intelligible given the subject's judgment that it is morally right to φ – for example, trying to induce a desire in oneself to φ, reproaching oneself for not having φ-ied or encouraging others to φ. Hence, on (1c) the motivation connected with moral judgment need not be to perform the act which is judged right. Offhand, (1c) seems to be both more plausible than (1) and supportive of moral non-cognitivism.

Another way of weakening (1) is to allow for occasions on which moral judgements have no motivational effect while insisting that the class of judgments, considered as such, is necessarily related to motivation. Thus, for example:

> (1d) Necessarily, it is normally the case that, when a person judges that it is morally right to φ, she is motivated to φ.

One might relativise this claim to a language community:

> (1e) Necessarily, it is normally the case that, when a person within the language community, L, judges that it is morally right to φ, she is motivated to φ.[14]

Unlike (1d), (1e) allows for persons who are not normally motivated when they make moral judgments. Unlike (1e), (1d) allows for persons who make moral judgments even if members of their language community are not normally motivated by their own moral judgments. These two weaker forms of internalism are not obviously consistent with – let alone supportive of – noncognitivism.

I now turn to the sort of internalism defended by Michael Smith. Smith's internalism is weaker than the standard kind stated in (1), but it differs from (1c-e). It can be stated as follows:

> (2) Necessarily, if a person judges that it is morally right that she φ-ies, that person is either motivated to φ or practically irrational.

This is clearly weaker than (1). It allows for the possibility of moral judgement without the associated motivation where the agent is practically irrational.

The notions of *judging*, of *being motivated* to φ, and of *practical irrationality* need clarification. I shall concentrate mainly on the latter. Judging, for Smith, involves the sort of mental state one is in when one subscribes to a moral evaluation. Smith does not presuppose that this mental state is a cognitive one (although this is what he in fact believes): the phrase 'a person judges that ...' is intended to be neutral between internalists and externalists.[15] Equally, the relevant judgement need not be publicly expressed. In deploying the claim that someone is motivated to φ, Smith seems to have in mind something slightly stronger than what internalists normally envisage. In particular, being motivated to φ requires more than an inclination to φ, since the agent must also believe that she has a normative reason to φ.[16] Intuitively, it would seem that these two states are independent.[17] I could be motivated to do what I believe at the time I have no reason to do. For example, in the heat of an argument an active, non-conscious desire might motivate me to hurt Bob's feelings even though I think I have no reason to do this.[18] Similarly, I can believe that I have reason to do something which I am not in the least inclined to do.

Let us turn now to the concept of practical irrationality. This topic will occupy me for the rest of this section. Unfortunately, Smith does not provide a clear account of the practical irrationality figuring in (2). What he has in mind is, first of all, weakness of will. In *The Moral Problem* he says: "agents who judge it right to act in certain ways are so motivated, and necessarily so, absent the distorting influences of weakness of will and other similar forms of practical unreason on their motivation".[19] The idea of *similar forms* of practical unreason is both crucial and unexplained here. Since Smith believes that to judge that one is morally required to perform some act is to judge that one has a normative reason to perform it, it might be suggested that all cases in which agents are not motivated to perform acts they judge to be morally right can be captured under the rubric of similar forms of practical unreason. Unfortunately, this suggestion seems misguided in at least two ways.

First, it seems to render (2) trivially true. For if Smith treats anyone who is not motivated to perform an act that she judges morally right to perform as practically irrational, (2) is a tautology. Indeed, characterised in this way internalism seems to amount to the claim that, necessarily, if a person judges that it is morally right that she φ-ies, that person is motivated to φ or is not. On some views of philosophical analysis this would render (2) uninteresting. Smith, however, rejects such views. He believes that philosophical analysis consists in rendering explicit the often tacit know-how that constitutes possession of a concept.[20] Hence, he might retort that (2) states an *unobvious* a priori, necessary truth. Whether this is so remains to be seen.

Second, it is not clear that what Smith has in mind here is what philosophers normally have in mind when they refer to 'weakness of will'. Action theorists generally use this phrase to indicate cases where an agent fails to do what he judges to be *best all things considered* to do.[21] But this is not what is presently at stake. For Smith nowhere makes the claim that, in judging that it is right to φ, an agent judges that it is best all things considered to φ. Moreover, suppose I perform an act that I judge to be best. Suppose further that I judge other acts to be morally right – and hence, according to Smith, that I judge that I have a pro tanto reason to perform these acts. Finally, suppose that I am not motivated to perform the latter acts. In these circumstances it is far from clear that I suffer from weakness of will, or indeed any other form of practical irrationality.

Even setting aside these two problems, (2) seems insufficiently discriminating to capture Smith's real view. It seems safe to assume that Smith would not take *all* forms of weakness of will to permit an agent to judge that it is morally right to ϕ and yet not be motivated to ϕ. Consider the following two cases:

> Example 1: A judges that it is morally right that she ϕ-ies, that she has reason, all things considered, to ψ and not to ϕ, and displays weakness of will in that she does not ψ. Nor does she ϕ.

> Example 2: B judges that it is morally right that she ϕ-ies, that she has reason, all things considered, to ψ, and does ψ and, hence, does not display weakness of will.

In the first of these examples, Smith's internalism accommodates the possibility of A making a moral judgment even where she is not motivated in the least to ϕ. At least, it will do this unless it is confined to specific kinds of weakness of will. In the second example, Smith's internalism rules out the possibility of B making a moral judgment where she is not motivated in the least to ϕ.

(2) seems unsatisfactory given that the ground for ascribing weakness of will to A and withholding it from B has nothing to do with whether they are motivated to do what they consider morally right – in that regard they do not differ – but depends entirely on whether they are motivated to perform a *different* act which they judge, all things considered, to be best but not morally right. For unless certain sources of irrationality are excluded (2) is consistent with the possibility that B makes a moral judgment and A does not.

Now consider the following refinement of (2):

> (2*) Necessarily, if a person judges that it is morally right that she ϕ-ies, that person is either motivated to ϕ or practically irrational in virtue of not being motivated to ϕ when she thinks it is morally right to ϕ.

This claim avoids the present problem. Since neither A nor B is motivated to do what they consider right, both of them are irrational in virtue of not doing what they consider right if either of them is. Hence, (2*) leaves no room for the claim that A, but not B, makes a moral judgment.

There is, however, one obvious problem with this reading. It does not square well with Smith's analysis of practical rationality. According to Smith, I have a reason to perform an act if my fully rational self would want me – my actual self – to perform it. Moreover, moral requirements are, according to Smith, requirements of reason. But if this is so, the mere fact that I am not inclined to perform an act that I think it is morally right to perform does not imply that my fully rational self would want me to perform it. For I might be wrong in thinking that I am morally required to perform the act. So how, on Smith's account, could I be irrational *in virtue of* not being motivated to perform an act I think it is morally right that I perform?[22] It is hard to avoid the impression that Smith appeals at this point to a feature of practical rationality which his own analysis of that rationality does not accommodate.

We can set this problem aside for a moment. For in fact (2*) does not adequately capture Smith's underlying view. (2*) is consistent with a person's being practically irrational in virtue of φ-ing when she thinks φ-ing is morally right; and Smith would surely reject this possibility. He would not, that is, contend that an agent is practically irrational in virtue of being motivated to perform an act that she thinks morally right. Hence, he must accept (2*) because he accepts (2**):

> (2**) Necessarily, if a person judges that it is morally right that she φ-ies, either: (a) that person is motivated to φ and not practically irrational in virtue of being so motivated; or (b) that person is practically irrational in virtue of not being motivated to φ when she thinks it is morally right to φ.

(2**) entails but is not entailed by (2*).[23] Moreover, I take it that if we reject (2**), then, in Smith's view, we have no reason to endorse (2*). For it is part and parcel of Smith's view of practical rationality – the view, I mean, underlying his endorsement of the second of the disjuncts in the consequent of (2**) – that one is not practically irrational in virtue of performing an act that one thinks morally right. So if we reject (2**), we must do so because we reject the conception of practical rationality which underlies Smith's endorsement of (2*).

The noteworthy thing about (2**) is that it makes it abundantly clear that what is at stake here is a certain view of the norms of practical rationality and not a view about philosophical psychology. As I mentioned earlier, externalism is often defined as the negation of internalism. Given (2**), an externalist so defined might think that, necessarily, if an agent judges that it is morally right to φ, that person will be motivated to φ. Such an externalist might think this, if she adds that the agent might be irrational in virtue of doing what she judges morally right! Yet the former view is normally taken to be the position within philosophical psychology held by internalists and appealed to by non-cognitivists.[24] Hence, unlike standard formulations of internalism, neither (2) nor (2\*\*) implies, in combination with a Humean theory of motivation, that moral judgments express conative states. Rather, they imply something about the norms of practical rationality.[25] They imply that if you believe that it is morally right that you ϕ, then, on pain of irrationality, you must be motivated to ϕ. Accordingly, the significance of Smith's appeal to practical irrationality in (2) is hard to overemphasise.

### III. The bare appeal to the possibility of amoralism

Having described Smith's version of internalism I now turn to the question of whether we should accept it. Typically externalists argue against internalism as follows: they point to the existence of certain characters, such as psychopaths, who make moral judgments and yet are not motivated to act in accordance with these judgments. From this they infer that it is possible for someone to fail to be motivated by their moral judgments, i.e. to be what I, following standard usage in the literature, shall call an amoralist in this paper.[26] Hence, they conclude, internalism is false. Consider for instance the following observations of Svavarsdóttir's: "…there are those who consistently display moral indifference – people who concede, for example, that certain investment policies have morally problematic consequences, but who can readily and without compunction ignore that in their business decisions. There even seem to be moral subversives, people who intentionally and knowingly pursue what they acknowledge to be morally wrong or bad, and do so for that very reason".[27] Alternatively, externalists describe amoralist psychological profiles that they then contend are possible (whether or not someone in fact has that profile). From this they infer that amoralism is possible.[28]

Smith rejects such appeals to the possibility of amoralist characters. He believes that amoralists "try to make moral judgments but fail".[29] Smith concedes that this may seem like an ad hoc move one would endorse only to save internalism. To explain why this is not so he points to what he thinks is a structural identity between the dispute between internalists and externalists and the dispute between those who claim that mastery of colour concepts presuppose colour experiences and those who deny that:[30] the attempt to refute internalism by appealing to the amoralist is structurally similar to the attempt to refute the view that mastery of colour terms requires colour experiences by appealing to the mastery of colour terms by people who can "reliably say 'Grass is green', 'Fire-engines are red', and so on", but are completely blind and, thus, have no colour experiences.[31] Smith believes that the latter attempt is unsuccessful: "the objection simply assumes the conclusion it is supposed to be arguing for"; it begs the question.[32]

There are several disputable elements in Smith's reply. First, a small point. It is not clear in general that one can rebut a charge of ad hocness by showing that the one who puts forward the charge begs the question. To make an ad hoc claim is, roughly, to make an assumption for which one has no independent warrant in order to save one's theory in face of what would otherwise be counter-evidence. To beg the question is, roughly, to put forward an argument where the addressee "believes one of the premises only because he already believes the conclusion or … would believe one of the premises only if he already believed the conclusion".[33] Now surely the fact that one would acknowledge the possibility of amoralism only if one already accepted externalism fails to show that Smith has independent warrant for adopting the 'try-but-fail' account of the utterances of the putative amoralist.

Second, Smith claims that Brink's appeal to the amoralist begs the question against internalism; but this claim is puzzling in view of how Smith himself dismisses strong generic internalism, i.e. (1a). Smith dismisses strong internalism on the ground that weakness of will is possible. In doing so he appeals to Stocker: "Lack of [the desire to do what one believes to be good] is commonplace. Through spiritual or physical tiredness, through accidie, through…despair,… one may feel less and less motivated to seek what is good".[34] But if the externalist's appeal to the amoralist begs the question against internalists, why does not Smith's appeal to Stocker's characters beg the question against the strong internalist? It seems that Smith has deprived himself of grounds for resisting the strong internalist's claim that people who do not act in accordance with their purported moral judgments try but fail to make moral judgments. So *either* Smith has no argument against strong internalism (or, if you like, he has one but it begs the question) *or* he has one against strong internalism but cannot dismiss Brink's appeal to the amoralist as question-begging.

Neither of the criticisms above addresses the intrinsic merit of Smith's charge that the appeal to amoralism begs the question. This is what I want to consider now. Charges of begging the question are tricky and, even if successful, it is often unclear what is thereby achieved. Specifically, it seems that some question-begging arguments render it reasonable for the addressee to accept the conclusion. Consider a case in which B denies and A affirms that it snowed last year. A then offers the following argument to B: "It snowed on Christmas Eve last year. Hence, it snowed last year." It might be true that B rejects the premise *only because* he rejects the conclusion and, hence, that the argument begs the question. But if, say, B has an independent memory of whether it snowed last year on Christmas Eve which he unreasonably fails to consult, then the argument does render the conclusion reasonable for him to accept even if it begs the question. The general point here is that the mere fact that one's acceptance of the negation of the conclusion commits one to reject at least one premise of a valid argument in its support does not justify the charge of begging the question, let alone the charge of the argument's not giving the addressee a reason to accept the conclusion. A question-begging argument may render it reasonable for the addressee to accept the conclusion if the following three conditions are satisfied: 1) the addressee of the argument has reasons independent of the conclusion to accept the premises of the argument; 2) the addressee of the argument fails to conduct his reasoning on the basis of these reasons; and 3) the reasons for which the addressee rejects (or accepts) the conclusion are bad ones.[35]

Let us return now to Smith's response to the externalist appeal to amoralism. His accusation that this appeal begs the question against internalists is inadequately supported by the claim that internalists are committed to denying the possibility of amoralism. The support is insufficient for the simple reason that, given Smith's definition of internalism in (2), internalists can acknowledge the possibility of amoralism. For as we saw in the last section, Smith's internalism is (or is based on) the view about norms of practical irrationality expressed in (2**). Accordingly, internalists can simply say that amoralists are practically irrational. This will allow them to concede that amoralists use moral terms competently and hence avoid the ad hoc reply that they try but fail to make moral judgments. For, given (2), a practically irrational person may be a competent user of moral language, judge that some course of conduct is morally right, and yet not be in the least motivated to perform it. Nor has Smith shown that internalists have considered the whole range of conceptually possible psychological profiles. Nor, consequently, has he shown that externalist appeals to such profiles are unable to raise genuine doubts about internalism.[36]

Note that I am not claiming that the appeal to amoralist profiles *cannot* beg the question against an internalist. Arguments do not beg the question *as such*. They beg the question when used in particular contexts for the benefit of particular addressees.[37] An argument that begs the question against me, may not beg the question against you. I may accept one of the premises because I accept the conclusion, whereas you may have independent grounds for accepting the premises. Thus even though some internalists may deny that the psychological profiles appealed to by externalists can involve competence with moral terms because they endorse internalism, Smith certainly has not shown that the appeal to the amoralist begs the question against all internalists. Nor has he shown that it is unreasonable to beg the question should such internalists exist.

Does this last criticism overlook Smith's analogy between the dispute about competence with colour terms and the dispute between internalists and externalists? I do not think so. Given the present account of question-begging arguments, the fact that these disputes involve arguments with the same logical form (that is to say: actually, Fa; therefore it is possible that there exists an x which is F) is irrelevant to the issue at hand. Whether or not an argument begs the question is not determined by its logical form, but by the inferential structure of the addressee's beliefs. Consider an appeal to the intelligibility of a science-fiction story of someone who through some technical device can 'feel' colours through her skin. Perhaps none of us has any beliefs about this case which are not in some way based on a prior theoretical belief about the necessary conditions for mastery of colour terms. At any rate, the appeal might well beg the question unreasonably against those who think that the having of colour experiences is a necessary condition of mastery of colour terms. By contrast, an appeal to well-known cases of, say, psychopathy will beg no questions unreasonably or otherwise against internalists, because all of us believe pre-theoretically that psychopaths are not motivated by their moral judgments.

To summarise the conclusions of this section: First, even if appeals to the amoralist are question-begging, it does not follow that the internalist's claim that amoralists try unsuccessfully to make moral judgments is not ad hoc. Second, Smith's rejection of the appeal to the amoralist sits uneasily with his own dismissal of strong internalism. Third, Smith has offered no compelling reasons to think that the appeal to the amoralist is question-begging, let alone unreasonably so. If these conclusions are correct, it must be concluded that Smith has failed to deal adequately with the externalist here.

## IV. An argument for the possibility of amoralism

I shall argue now that externalists can provide positive support for the claim that amoralism is possible. The support I have in mind, moreover, involves assumptions that are plausible independently of the dispute between internalists and externalists about moral judgment. The essential claims are as follows:[38]

> 3. It is possible for someone to judge – whether truly or not – that (a) moral requirements include impartial other-regarding obligations which do not apply to agents in virtue of their own aims or interests; (b) that rational action is action that achieves the agent's aims or promotes her interests; and (c) that fulfilling other-regarding obligations often will not advance the agent's aims and interests.
>
> 4. If (3), then it is possible for someone to judge both that she is morally required to $\phi$ and that it is irrational to $\phi$.
>
> 5. Hence, it is possible for someone to judge both that she is morally required to $\phi$ and that it is irrational to $\phi$.
>
> 6. If (5), then it is possible for someone to judge that she is morally required to $\phi$ and yet not be motivated to $\phi$.
>
> 7. Hence, it is possible for someone to judge that she is morally required to $\phi$ and yet not be motivated to $\phi$.

As I say, these claims are independent of the theoretical commitments of internalists and externalists. Claim (3) is true for the simple reason that some people have in fact believed (a)-(c), whether rightly or not. Claim (4) is true for the equally simple reason that some of these people have seen the relevant entailment of (a)-(c). And claim (6) is true, it seems, if it is possible for judgments about what one has reason not to do to influence what one is motivated to do.

This argument need not worry Smith, however. True, the inference is impeccable and the conclusion flatly contradicts generic internalism of the kind described in (1). But Smith's internalism is consistent with (7), because it is consistent with someone's not being in the least motivated by her moral judgments where she is irrational. So to threaten Smith's internalism we need to make the following alteration:

> (6\*) If (5), then it is possible for someone to judge that she is morally required to $\phi$ and yet be neither motivated to $\phi$ nor practically irrational.

(7*) Hence, it is possible for someone to judge that she is morally required to φ and yet be neither motivated to φ nor practically irrational.

(6*) is plausible, because if an agent reasonably judges that it would be irrational of her to do what she judges she is morally required to do, then it is not clear what sort of irrationality she would display in not doing what she judges to be irrational. In fact, (6*) is more plausible than Smith's internalism. For the strongest argument in favour of internalism about moral judgments is based on two things: internalism about reason judgment (i.e. the view that one is either motivated to do what one judges that one has reason to do or practically irrational), and the assumption that in making a self-addressed, future-directed moral judgment one makes a reason judgment. In any case, Smith grounds his defence of internalism about moral judgments on an appeal to internalism about reason judgments.[39] (7*) is inconsistent with Smith's internalism.

It is not entirely clear to me how Smith should respond to this argument. He might want to reject (5), and presumably (4). For according to Smith, the belief that one is morally required to φ simply is the belief that one would want oneself to φ if one were fully rational (where the conduct picked out by 'φ' is of an appropriate sort such as something promoting the welfare of others). Call this the "belief identity claim".[40] Such identities may not be transparent to the believer. It may require a good deal of philosophical analysis to see the truth of the relevant identity claim. So presumably Smith would want to say that the revised argument shows merely that people can falsely believe that they judge that they are morally required to φ and yet consider it irrational to φ. The argument does not show that this is what they in fact do.

I am not persuaded by this reply. First, it is not clear that Smith is entitled to offer it. For in his view the task of someone who analyses a concept (e.g. 'Colour') is to identify the remarks that surround this concept and which are treated as platitudinous by those who master the concept (e.g. 'The colours of objects cause us to see objects as coloured'). In doing this, one maps one's inferential dispositions. But if some philosophers do not think that the present sort of argument violates various platitudes, and if their inferential dispositions reflect this, then on Smith's own view of the nature of conceptual analysis, this will count against the idea that coming to master moral terms involves coming to treat as platitudinous that we have a reason to do what we are morally required to do.

Second, Smith's view that to judge that one is morally required to φ is to judge that one has reason to ϕ may be irrelevant to the issue of motivation here. For in the sort of case we have in mind, the agent is not only ignorant of this identity, but has a transparent belief that she has reason not to do what she judges morally required. Surely, in some cases this will mean that the agent fails to be motivated to do what she judges to be morally required. Hence, it is possible not to be motivated to do what you judge you ought to do, morally speaking.

In response, Smith might say that a person of this sort is irrational for at least two reasons. First, given the belief identity thesis such a person fails to desire what she non-transparently believes she would desire if she were fully rational, and this makes her irrational. Second, by her own lights, counting only transparent beliefs, it would be irrational of her to ϕ; and by her own lights, counting only her non-transparent beliefs, it would be rational of her to ϕ. Hence, she holds inconsistent beliefs. And even if the inconsistency is inaccessible to the agent, holding inconsistent beliefs, it might be claimed, always involves irrationality. So even if she is not motivated to act, this absence of motivation is consistent with Smith's internalism, at least if the present sorts of irrationality render the agent practically irrational (as opposed to theoretically irrational).

The crucial question here is how we are to understand Smith's appeal to practical irrationality in (2). Would the inconsistencies mentioned above render an agent practically irrational in Smith's sense? Would Smith agree that where an agent is host to merely inaccessible inconsistency, she need not be motivated?[41] In my view, there is a danger here that Smith's internalism will become far too weak. Consider the following kind of agent: one who occurrently believes both that he is morally required to ϕ and that he has reason to ϕ; who does not suffer from weakness of will; who holds the two mentioned beliefs irrationally because they contradict some of his justified, non-occurrent beliefs; and who is not motivated to ϕ. Internalists who offer positive answers to the above questions will be obliged to deny that this kind of agent constitutes a counterexample to Smith's internalism. And since we all hold non-transparently inconsistent beliefs, it seems that these internalists will be unable to explain the close connection between morality and motivation which, for many philosophers, is the attraction of internalism in the first place.[42] That is a high price to pay. Indeed it is so high that it would probably be better not to pay at all – better to continue to regard the revised argument for the possibility of amoralism stated in (3)-(7*) as sound.

## V. The reliable connection argument

The previous two sections assess Smith's attack on the main argument for externalism. In the present section I want to review his positive case for internalism. I begin with what might be called the reliable connection argument. This takes the following claim as its point of departure:

> (8) There is a reliable connection in good and strong-willed persons between changes in moral judgments and changes in motivation.[43]

According to Smith, internalists and externalists alike must offer some account of this striking truth; and as he sees it, only internalists can provide a plausible explanation. This is a reason for accepting internalism.

Internalists can explain (8) because it follows straightforwardly from internalism. A person who is good and strong-willed is not practically irrational. It follows from internalism – that is, from (2) – that if this kind of person judges it right to $\phi$, then she will be motivated to $\phi$. Rationalists like Smith think that this is due to the fact that the belief that it is right to $\phi$ causes a desire de re to $\phi$.

Externalists obviously cannot explain (8) by appealing to a necessary connection between moral judgment and motivation.[44] Instead they must appeal to the claim that a good and strong-willed person has a de dicto desire to do what is right: they must maintain that a good and strong-willed person desires that if some action is right, then she will perform that action. The corresponding de re desire to do what is right can be expressed as follows: there are acts which are right and, for all such acts, A desires to perform them. Hence, on the externalist account good and strong-willed persons are persons who desire to do acts that are right whichever they happen to be. No wonder their motivation tracks their changing moral views.

In Smith's view, the externalist explanation in terms of a de dicto desire to what is right is flawed because it implies that the virtuous person has no underived desires – no de re desires – to do what is right. But, says Smith, it is a platitude that virtuous persons have such desires. Virtuous persons desire to perform right actions because of their right-making features and not simply to perform acts that are right whatever they may be. Paraphrasing Bernard Williams, Smith accuses the externalist of providing the virtuous person with one thought too many. Since the internalist explanation is to be preferred to the externalist one, we should endorse the internalist account of mastery of moral terms: "amoralists do not have mastery of moral terms, and they therefore do not really make moral judgments".[45]

In my view there are several objections to this argument. First, does Smith show that it is a platitude, or even true, that good and strong-willed persons do not have a de dicto desire to do what is right?[46] To support this claim Smith appeals to a well-known example, devised by Fried, which Williams has used against moral theories in which the notion of impartiality plays an important role.[47] In this example we are asked to imagine a person who can either save his wife or a stranger and is motivated to save his wife partly by the thought that it is morally permissible for him to do so. In Williams' view, to be so motivated is to have "one thought too many" and Smith suggests that virtuous persons, as construed by externalists, suffer from a similar flaw. Suppose Williams is right. From this nothing follows about cases in which an agent revises his values, let alone his fundamental values. For Williams' case is simply not a case of this sort and it is not clear why Williams' critical point about an agent who is motivated not by an underived desire to save his wife but an underived desire to do what is right applies to cases involving revision of fundamental commitments.[48]

Second, it is not clearly true, let alone a platitude, that good and strong-willed persons lack a de dicto desire to do what is right.[49] The reliable connection argument is supposed to support a conceptual truth. It cannot do this if the platitude about virtuous persons appealed to is not a conceptual truth. In my view, however, the platitude is not a truth at all, and a fortiori not a conceptual truth. Before he develops new de re desires to do what he now believes is morally right, a good and strong-willed agent who has recently revised his fundamental values may well be properly motivated by his de dicto desire to do what is right.[50] Moreover, the de dicto desire to do what is morally right need not always be manifest in the agent's conscious reasoning – Smith has argued most desires do not – but might instead act as a kind of filter on what motivations we develop.[51] Yet, if the desire rarely appears in conscious thought it is hard to see why the possession of it should render one's motivational structure fetishistic.

Third, the reliable connection argument would not show Smith's internalism to be more attractive than other forms of internalism. Consider the target of Smith's reliable connection argument, namely externalism. I take it that, for Smith, externalism simply involves the rejection of internalism as he characterises it, i.e. denial of the following claim:

(2) Necessarily, if a person judges that it is morally right that she ϕ-ies, that person is either motivated to ϕ or practically irrational.

The "either…or" here can be read as an exclusive or an inclusive disjunction. If the former, then a view normally seen as a stronger version of internalism than the one defended by Smith qualifies as externalist, namely:

(9) Necessarily, if a person judges that it is morally right that she ϕ-ies, that person is motivated to ϕ.

For consider a case in which an agent judges that it is morally right that she ϕ-ies, ϕ-ies, and yet is practically irrational. Such a case will refute (2) but not (9) if the "either ... or" in (2) is exclusive. To define externalism as the negation of a dichotomous (2) is therefore to imply that (9) is an externalist position!

This unwelcome implication suggests that we should read the "either ... or" as inclusive. But on this reading Smith runs into a different problem. For (9) – which would then qualify as internalist – explains the reliable connection between changes in moral judgment and motivation if (2) does. Hence, the reliable connection argument provides no reason to prefer Smith's weak version of internalism to the stronger form stated in (9).[52]

Smith might reply that although the reliable connection argument is neutral between different forms of internalism, there are independent reasons for preferring his own, weaker internalism. For instance, Smith thinks that strong forms of internalism such as (9) are shown to be "manifestly implausible" by Michael Stocker's examples of depressed or apathetic persons who judge some act right and yet have little motivation to perform it.[53] However, as I have already argued this appeal combines uneasily with Smith's own dismissal of the externalist's appeal to amoralism. Smith makes room for the reliable connection argument in the first place by dismissing the externalist appeal to amoralists as question-begging. But if this dismissal is warranted, then surely a similar, strong internalist's dismissal of Smith's appeal to Stocker's apathetic figures as question-begging is as well. Hence, either Smith does not reject the externalist appeal to amoralism as question-begging, in which case he must face this appeal directly, or he does, in which case his argument for internalism does not favour his own version of internalism. Since I do not consider the externalist appeal to amoralism question-begging, I think Smith should opt for the first horn of this dilemma. Taking this option, however, he would need to show that it is "a fact of ordinary moral experience" that Stocker's characters are possible, but not "a fact of ordinary moral experience" that the characters appealed to by externalists are possible.

Fourth, externalists can in any case explain the reliable connection without appealing to a de dicto desire to do what is right.[54] There are at least two ways they can do so. First, externalism is consistent with the claim that it is contingently true of some persons that whenever they believe that they are morally required to φ, they believe that they have a reason to φ. Since externalists about moral judgment and motivation may be internalists about reason judgments and motivation, they might say that whenever such persons believe that they are morally required to perform some act, they believe that they have a reason to and are therefore motivated to perform it. If good and strong-willed persons are such persons, then externalists can explain why good and strong-willed persons' motivation reliably follows their moral judgments without appealing to a de dicto desire to do whatever is morally right. Second, we might think of a good and strong-willed agent as someone who has a number of non-derivative desires whose content is quite broad: to see justice done.[55] That this person's motivation reliably tracks his view about what is just is not the sort of fortuitous shadowing by motivation of moral judgment that a reliable connection seems to require if we ascribe to virtuous and strong-willed agents desires with very narrow content only. True, in cases in which the agent changes his fundamental views about morality, the very general desires would have to change. But, as I have argued, in such cases it is unclear why a virtuous person would not – or necessarily would not – be guided by her judgments about what is morally right.

Fifth, it can be denied that externalism needs to figure in the explanation of the reliable connection. Externalists can claim that the reliable connection obtains simply in virtue of the meaning given to the phrase 'good and strong-willed persons'. It is part of what Smith means by calling someone a good and strong-willed person that her motivation tracks her moral judgments.[56]

In view of these objections it seems fair to conclude that Smith's reliable connection argument for (2)-type internalism is unsound. Smith offers another argument in favour of internalism, however, and it is to this that I shall now turn.

## VI. The appeal to rationalism about moral requirements

Like Kant, Smith endorses rationalism about moral requirements:

> (10) If it is right for agents to φ in circumstances C, then there is reason for those agents to φ in C.[57]

Smith's claims that (10) is true in virtue of our very concept of a moral requirement. He also believes that there are in fact moral requirements. He offers two arguments for (10). The first is that we can make sense of the fact that we morally approve or disapprove of others – as opposed to morally "like" or morally "dislike" others – only if we assume both that those of whom we approve or disapprove are rational agents and that moral requirements are requirements of rationality.[58] The second begins with the observation that we expect rational agents to do what they are morally required to do; claims that we are entitled to hold this expectation only if moral requirements apply to agents in virtue of their being rational; and concludes that moral requirements are requirements of rationality.[59]

Smith thinks that rationalism entails internalism. If this is correct we can appeal to rationalism to defend internalism:

> (11) A judges that it is morally right for her to φ in C.

> (12) An agent's judgment that it is morally right for her to φ in C is identical to her belief that, if she were fully rational, she would want herself to φ in C (the belief identity claim).

> (13) Hence, A believes that if she were fully rational, she would want herself to φ in C.

> (14) Hence, if A does not have a desire to φ in C, she lacks a desire that she believes she would have if she were fully rational.

> (15) If an agent lacks a desire that she believes she would have if she were fully rational, she is practically irrational by her own lights and, thus, practically irrational (the 'irrationality of incoherence doctrine').

> (16) Hence, if A does not have a desire to φ in C, she is practically irrational.

> (17) Hence, if an agent believes that it is morally right for her to φ in C, she is either motivated (i.e. has a desire) to φ in C or practically irrational.

The two crucial premises in this argument are the belief identity claim and the irrationality of incoherence doctrine. To support the former Smith presses into service the view of philosophical analysis we encountered above – the view, that is, on which philosophical analysis can uncover unobvious identities. In support of the second premise Smith claims that failing to desire what one judges desirable involves psychological incoherence amounting to irrationality.[60]

I am not persuaded by this argument. First, David Copp has convincingly argued that the belief identity claim and the irrationality of incoherence claim are not cotenable: if one is true, the other is not. His thought is this. If agents can have inaccessible beliefs and desires, there need not be anything irrational about not desiring what one judges desirable. Copp's example is: Lois Lane believes that Clark Kent works in the office next door, and she believes that it is not the case that Superman is in the office next door. But given Smith's belief identity claim, and given that Clark Kent is Superman, Lois Lane's belief that Clark Kent works in the office next door simply is her belief that Superman is in the office next door. Hence, given the way she holds her beliefs, she has the inaccessible belief that Superman is in the office next door. Taking into account accessible as well as inaccessible beliefs, Lois Lane holds inconsistent beliefs. But this does not automatically make her irrational, for she might have no reason to think that Clark Kent is Superman. Similarly, there might be nothing irrational about lacking a desire that one inaccessibly believes that one would have if one were fully rational.[61] The upshot of this is that either the belief identity claim is false, or the irrationality of incoherence doctrine is false, or the argument is invalid because 'belief' is used in different senses in (12) and (15).

Second, the irrationality of incoherence doctrine is hard to reconcile with Smith's own account of normative reasons. According to Smith:

> (19) A has a normative reason to φ in C, if and only if A's fully rational self would want A to φ in C.

But if we accept this analysis it becomes doubtful that it is necessarily irrational not to desire to do what one judges desirable. For suppose I believe falsely that I am morally required to φ. It does not follow from Smith's account of normative reasons that I have a normative reason to φ, since my fully rational self might not want my actual self to φ. The upshot of this is that Smith's own account of normative reasons is incompatible with the irrationality of incoherence doctrine.

Smith has, however, tried to meet this challenge. He suggests that on "the plausible assumption that the agent's fully rational self desires that the psychology of her less than fully rational self is as coherent as possible she will want her less than fully rational self to desire that she φs in C... Agents thus quite generally have a reason to desire in accordance with their evaluative beliefs".[62] But it is by no means clear that this follows (nor indeed why our fully rational self wants our actual self's psychology to be as coherent as possible). For the relation in question – the relation between the evaluative belief and desire at issue – is only one determinant, as Smith himself sees it, of the overall coherence of the agent's psychology.[63] Other determinants include the relation between the relevant desire and other desires the agent has. It may well be, then, that desiring in accordance with one's evaluative beliefs will decrease the overall coherence of one's psychology. Hence, Smith has failed to defeat the second objection.

Third, it can be argued that the irrationality of incoherence doctrine is suspect. There is a difference between the closest possible world in which I am fully rational and the closest possible world in which I am fully rational and all the desires I have are desires that I have in virtue of being fully rational. In the former world, unlike the latter, I may have desires that I am rationally permitted but not rationally required to have; and it is this world that Smith asks us to consider. One's fully rational self might therefore have a desire that one does not have in virtue of being fully rational and it is not clear why such desires have any normative force. One cannot infer, then, from a person's belief that she would have a certain desire if she were fully rational that that person believes that she is irrational for not having this desire.[64]

Fourth, the challenge to the irrationality of incoherence doctrine presented above is easily transformed into a direct challenge to internalism itself. For suppose an agent judges that it is morally right to φ in C. Suppose that the agent is wrong. It is morally wrong to φ in C. According to Smith's account of moral wrongness, this implies that the agent's fully rational self would want her not to φ in C. In some such cases, the agent's fully rational self will want her actual self not to be motivated to φ. According to Smith's account of rationality, this in turn implies that she has a reason not to be motivated to φ in C.

Hence, it appears that she is not irrational in not being motivated to φ in C. In other words, on Smith's account of normative reasons it seems to follow that internalism is false.[65]

## VII. Conclusion

If the appeal to the possibility of amoralism supports externalism despite Smith's reservations, and if neither the reliable connection argument nor the rationalist defence of internalism succeeds, one might reasonably wonder what makes internalism seem attractive. Here it is important to note first that very different sources lie behind different kinds of internalism. In explaining the attraction of internalism Jonathan Dancy, for instance, points to the intuition that "it would be odd for someone to say 'This action is wrong but I don't see that as at all relevant to my choice'".[66] This intuition, Dancy says, can be backed up "by the thought that moral considerations are ones whose practical relevance cannot be escaped by saying 'I don't care about that sort of thing'".[67] These reflections differ and support different sorts of position. Neither supports internalism in Michael Smith's sense. The second expresses the view that moral norms are categorical. The first supports the view that there is an internal relation between moral judgments and judgments about what one has a normative reason to do. But this in itself does not support internalism about moral judgments. For there might not be an internal relation between judgments about what one has a normative reason to do, on the one hand, and being either motivated to act accordingly or practically irrational, on the other.

This brings us back to where we started: the intimate connection between moral judgment and motivation. Most internalists are struck by the oddness of someone's not being motivated to act in accordance with self-addressed moral judgments. But we should note two things here. First, Smith's internalism is consistent with the denial of any strong tendency to be so motivated. It comfortably accommodates our being disposed to practical irrationality and hence systematic failure to act in accordance with our moral judgments. Second, externalists can accommodate the existence of an intimate connection between moral judgment and motivation. They can claim that it is odd for motivation not to track moral judgment just as it is odd for snow to fall in summer: there is a strong contingent association between motivation and moral judgment. It is true, moreover, that someone who expresses her moral views publicly will generally be motivated to act in accordance with those views.[68]

## Notes

1. I am grateful to Nils Holtug and Paisley Livingston for useful comments on an earlier draft of this article.
2. "We expect people who accept moral claims or make moral judgments to act in certain ways", Brink 1989, p. 37; "To think that you ought to do something is to be motivated to do it", Harman 1977, p. 33; "When we are conscious that an action is *fit* to be done, or that it *ought* to be done, it is not conceivable that we can remain *uninfluenced*, or want a *motive* to action", Price 1974, p. 186; "*Believing I should* seems to bring with it *my being motivated to* – at least absent weakness of will and the like", Smith, 1994, p. 60.
3. Important defences of internalism include: Hare 1952; Korsgaard 1986; McDowell 1985; Nagel 1970; Smith 1994, esp. pp. 60-91.
4. Blackburn 1984, p. 188; Hume 1739-40, Book III, Part I, Section I; Stevenson 1937, p. 13; Stroud 1977, p. 172.
5. Apart from Smith 1994 see, for instance, Smith 1999; Smith 1997; Smith 1996a.
6. See Brink 1989, p. 42; Svavarsdóttir 1999, p. 182. I am not claiming that the three possibilities mentioned here are exhaustive.
7. Throughout this article, statements of the form 'A judges that it is morally right to $\phi$' are to be interpreted elliptically as equivalent to 'A judges that it is morally right that she $\phi$-ies'.
8. Internalists might require some sort of hypothetical motivation to obtain in cases such as this. E.g., they might insist that if it were now the case that the agent believed that she could make it more likely that she would $\phi$ later by $\psi$-ing now, she would now be motivated to $\psi$. However, this will not do. For while an agent of whom this is true is now disposed to be motivated to $\phi$, it need not be the case that he or she is now (dispositionally) motivated to $\phi$.
9. Russ Shafer-Landau, for instance, defines externalism as the negation of Michael Smith's internalism: see Shafer-Landau 1998, p. 353, n. 1. This implies that the view that, necessarily, if a person judges that it is morally right that she $\phi$-ies, that person is motivated not to $\phi$ or practically irrational, is an externalist position.
10. For a position analogous to the one I take here see Tenenbaum 2000, p. 110. It is hard to deny that there are necessary and *un*interesting connections between moral judgment and motivation – e.g. that, necessarily, if an agent judges that it is right for her to $\phi$, then if she has reason all things considered to $\phi$ she will be motivated to $\phi$ unless she is irrational. See Lillehammer 1997, p. 194.
11. Richard Hare is the exception here. See Hare 1993, esp. pp. 67-85 and Hare 1981, pp. 20-4.
12. See, for instance, Smith 1994, p. 61. For an influential description of some of these supposed counterexamples to (1a) see Stocker 1979, p. 741.
13. Audi 1997, p. 138. Ingmar Persson draws a parallel distinction between the claim that a motivating reason itself partly consists in a desire and the claim that the state of having a motivating reason partly consists in a desire: see Persson 1996, p. 145.
14. For related positions see Blackburn 1995, p. 48; Lenman 1999; Tenenbaum 2000; Dreier 1990.
15. See Svavarsdóttir 1999, p. 167n. William K. Frankena suggests that while there might be a sense of 'accept' in which one cannot accept a moral obligation without having some motivation to fulfil it, it is logically possible that one might recognise a moral claim as true and yet not be moved by it: see Frankena 1958, p. 66. There might be something like a "mere intellectual apprehension" of a moral truth. Like Frankena, I take it that if this is so, externalism wins. Audi raises a similar point in Audi 1997, pp. 139-40.
16. Smith 1994, p. 185. According to Korsgaard internalists hold that, necessarily, if an agent judges that it is morally right that she $\phi$-ies, then she sees a "motive or reason for doing it": Korsgaard 1986, pp. 8-9. If, as I believe, it is possible to judge that one has a reason to do

something and yet not be inclined to do it, then Korsgaard's position, on that ground alone, differs from Smith's.
17. Richard J. Arneson helpfully distinguishes between three things a preference may involve: behavioural dispositions, experiences, and judgments about value: Arneson 1990, p. 162. He believes that these three elements are conceptually independent even if they often appear together. Smith agrees to the extent that he thinks that although some desires may involve experiences these are not what constitute the desire. See also Watson 1982.
18. I owe the example to Mele 1995, pp. 396-7.
19. Smith 1994, p. 61. Presumably Smith thinks that failing to desire those things that one believes one would desire if one were fully rational is another form of practical irrationality.
20. Smith 1994, pp. 29-32.
21. See, for instance, Audi 1993, pp. 319-33; Davidson 1980, pp. 21-42; Mele 1992, pp. 87, 122-4 and 230-4.
22. My argument here is similar to, but stronger than, an argument by Dreier 1996, p. 366. Unlike me, Dreier does not press Smith on the source of irrationality involved in not being motivated to perform an act that you believe it is morally right that you perform. See also Persson 1996, pp. 151-4 and Smith 1996b.
23. The latter is shown by the fact that (2\*\*) is vulnerable to a counterexample that would not refute (2\*), namely: a person is motivated to act in accordance with what he judges morally right and is irrational in virtue of this.
24. Hallvard Lillehammer, for instance, says that "[t]he resolution of [the dispute between internalists and externalists] has important consequences. For whereas the internalist can construe moral judgements either as non-cognitive states like desire or as cognitive states like belief, the externalist is committed to construe moral judgements as cognitive states like belief. A vindication of externalism would therefore lend support to those who believe in the possibility of some kind of moral reality", Lillehammer 1997, p. 187. This description is false if we regard externalists as deniers of (2\*\*). For such externalists may differ from internalists over practical rationality and agree with them on whether moral judgments express non-cognitive states.
25. Hence, Audi dubs the sort of internalism defended by Smith and Korsgaard "rational agent motivational internalism", Audi 1997, p.137. See also Svavarsdottir 1999, pp. 164-5.
26. Brink 1986, p. 30; Brink 1989, pp. 46-8; Svavarsdóttir 1999, pp. 161, 176-83.
27. Svavarsdóttir 1999, p. 161.
28. Brink 1986, p. 30.
29. Smith 1994, p. 68. Smith, however, rejects Hare's inverted commas reply to amoralists: see Hare 1952, pp. 124-6, 163-5.
30. Smith 1994, p. 69.
31. Smith 1994, p. 70.
32. Smith 1994, p. 70. For similar views see Dancy 1993, p. 5 and Lenman 1999, p. 444.
33. Sanford 1972, p. 198.
34. Stocker 1979, p. 741.
35. I discuss reasonable question-begging arguments more fully in Lippert-Rasmussen 2000 and Lippert-Rasmussen 2001
36. That internalists have failed to do so is claimed by Mele in Mele 1995, pp. 404-5. In Mele's view, if there are any pre-theoretical intuitions concerning the nature of beliefs and desires, these favour externalism. Strongly supportive of this is the case of persons who after the onset of depression or neurological damage continue "to make the same discriminations and judgments using moral terms but now without motivational effect", Brink 1997a, p. 24; Brink 1997b, p. 258.

37. Sanford 1981, pp. 145-58.
38. I am indebted here to Brink 1997a, p. 19.
39. Smith 1994, p. 60.
40. Copp 1997, p. 39.
41. Smith certainly seems to have a narrower notion of practical irrationality in mind. For he says "absent the distorting influences of weakness of will and other similar forms of practical unreason" (Smith 1994, p. 61), and an inaccessible inconsistency is hardly a *similar* form of unreason as weakness of will. As Brink interprets him, only cases where "indifference does not reflect principles the agent accepts" (Brink 1997a, p. 18) but rather concerns whether the result of practical deliberation is transformed into motivation or action involve the relevant sort of practical irrationality. I take it Brink has occurrent acceptance in mind here.
42. See Smith's own attempt to show how intuitively attractive internalism is, Smith 1994, pp. 60-1. Also, the argument that Smith provides in favour of internalism – the reliable connection argument – does not appear to support this very weak form of internalism against stronger forms, i.e. views according to which, necessarily, if an judges that it is morally right that she φ-ies and she does not suffer from weakness of will, she is motivated to φ (even if she suffers from other forms of irrationality, e.g. she has non-transparently inconsistent beliefs).
43. We can ignore for present purposes the question whether it is a platitude that a good and strong-willed persons' motivations tend to track her inaccessible as well as her accessible moral judgments.
44. As indicated in note 9, this claim is strictly speaking false if we take "externalism" to refer to the position held by those who reject (2), i.e. Smith's internalism.
45. Smith 1994, 76; Smith 1996b, p. 167. In Smith 1996c Smith offers a different version of the reliable connection argument. Although he offers it as a clarification of the argument put forward in *The Moral Problem* it is clearly different in that the explanans is not the motivational dispositions of good agents. For a discussion of this argument see Svavarsdóttir 1999, pp. 207-15.
46. Lillehammer 1997, p. 192; Svavarsdóttir 1999, p. 205.
47. Smith 1994, pp. 75-6; Williams 1981, pp. 17-19.
48. It is also noteworthy that several philosophers see a source of moral motivation to lie in a de dicto desire to do what is morally right. See, for instance, Prichard 1928, pp. 27-8 and Ross 1930, pp. 156-60. In the absence of further clarification of Smith's concept of a platitude, the fact that prominent moral philosophers have subscribed to such an account of moral motivation suggests that this account is not platitudinously false.
49. Lillehammer 1997, p. 191; Copp 1997, pp. 49-50; Noordhof 1999, p. 131.
50. Shafer-Landau 1998, p. 357.
51. Pettit and Smith 1990; Shafer-Landau 1998, p.357. For the idea of a filter on motivation see Railton 1984, pp. 134-71.
52. The same is true of an even stronger form of internalism, namely (1a) above: necessarily, if a person judges that it is morally right that she φ-ies, that person will φ.
53. Smith 1994, p. 61.
54. Lillehammer 1997, pp. 194-5; Copp 1997, pp. 50-1.
55. Shafer-Landau 1998, p. 356.
56. Lillehammer 1997, p. 193.
57. Smith 1994, p. 62. However, Smith's rationalism is weaker than Kant's: Smith merely claims that moral requirements entail a pro tanto reason, not an all things considered reason.
58. Smith 1994, pp. 87-90.
59. Smith 1994, pp. 85-7. We can, however, disregard the second argument in favour of rational-

ism in the present context, because Smith's internalism appears as a premise in the argument. (If Smith's second argument for rationalism were his only argument, then, he could not appeal to the claim that rationalism entails internalism to defend internalism.)
60. Smith 1994, p. 177.
61. Copp 1997, pp. 38-43.
62. Smith 1995, p. 127.
63. The concept of coherence at issue here may need clarification. It is unobvious what relations between desires and beliefs are relevant to the assessment of psychological coherence.
64. Pace Smith 1994, p. 177.
65. For a similar view see Shafer-Landau 1999, pp. 33-4.
66. Dancy 1993, p.4.
67. Dancy 1993, p.4.
68. Frankena 1958, pp. 68-9.

## References

Arneson, Richard J. (1990) "Liberalism, Distributive Subjectivism, and Equal Opportunity for Welfare", *Philosophy & Public Affairs*, 19, pp. 158-94.
Audi, Robert (1993) Weakness of Will and Rational Action, in: R. Audi, *Action, Intention, and Reason* (Ithaca: Cornell University Press), pp. 319-33.
Audi, Robert (1997) Moral Judgment and Reasons for Action, in: G. Cullity and B. Gaut (eds.), *Ethics and Practical Reason* (Oxford: Clarendon Press), pp. 125-59.
Blackburn, Simon (1984) *Spreading the Word* (Oxford: Oxford University Press).
Blackburn, Simon (1995) The Flight to Reality, in: R. Hursthouse, G. Lawrence, and W. Quinn (eds.), *Virtues and Reason* (Oxford: Clarendon Paperbacks), pp. 35-56.
Brink, David (1986) Externalist Moral Realism, *Southern Journal of Philosophy*, suppl. vol. 24, pp. 111-25.
Brink, David O. (1989) *Moral Realism and the Foundation of Ethics* (Cambridge: Cambridge University Press).
Brink, David (1997a) Moral Motivation", *Ethics*, 108, pp. 4-32.
Brink, David (1997b) Kantian Rationalism: Inescapability, Authority, and Supremacy, in: G. Cullity and B. Gaut (eds.) *Ethics and Practical Reason* (Oxford: Clarendon Press), pp. 255-91.
Copp, David (1997) Belief, Reason, and Motivation, *Ethics*, 108, pp. 33-54.
Dancy, Jonathan (1993) *Moral Reasons* (Oxford: Blackwell).
Davidson, Donald (1980) How is Weakness of will Possible?, in: D. Davidson, *Actions and Events* (Oxford, Clarendon Press), pp. 21-42.
Dreier, James (1990) Internalism and Speaker Relativism, *Ethics*, 101, pp. 6-26.
Dreier, James (1996) The Moral Problem, *Mind*, 105, pp. 363-7.
Frankena, William K. (1958) Obligation and Motivation in Recent Moral Philosophy, in: A. I. Melden (ed.) *Essays in Moral Philosophy* (Seattle: University of Washington Press), pp. 40-81.
Hare, Richard (1952) *The Language of Morals* (Oxford: Clarendon Press).
Hare, Richard (1963) *Freedom and Reason* (Oxford: Oxford University Press).
Hare, Richard (1981) *Moral Thinking: Its Levels, Method and Point* (Oxford: Oxford University Press).
Harman, Gilbert (1977) *The Nature of Morality* (Oxford: Oxford University Press).
Hume, David (1739-40) *A Treatise of Human Nature*.
Korsgaard, Christine (1986) Scepticism about Practical Reason, *Journal of Philosophy*, 83, pp. 5-25.

Lenman, James (1999) The Externalist and the Amoralist, *Philosophia*, 27, pp. 441-57.
Lillehammer, Hallvard (1997) Smith on Moral Fetishism, *Analysis*, 57.3, pp. 187-95.
Lippert-Rasmussen (2000) Irrationality, Inference, and Question-Begging Arguments, in: B. Brogaard (ed.), *Rationality and Irrationality*, Contributions of the Austrian Ludwig Wittgenstein Society, 8 (Kirchberg: Austrian Ludwig Wittgenstein Society), pp. 264-70.
Lippert-Rasmussen (2001) Are Question-Begging Arguments Necessarily Unreasonable?, *Philosophical Studies*, 104.2, pp. 123-41.
McDowell, John (1985) Values and Secondary Qualities, in: T. Honderich (ed.) *Morality and Objectivity* (Boston: Routledge & Kegan Paul, 1985), pp. 110-29.
Mele, Alfred R. (1992) *Springs of Action* (Oxford: Oxford University Press).
Mele, Alfred R. (1995) Motivation: Essentially Motivation-Constituting Attitudes, *Philosophical Review*, 104, pp. 387-423.
Nagel, Thomas (1970) *The Possibility of Altruism* (Princeton, Princeton University Press).
Noordhof, Paul (1999) Moral Requirements are still not rational Requirements, *Analysis*, 59, pp. 127-36.
Persson, Ingmar (1996) Critical notice of Michael Smith: The Moral Problem, *Theoria*, 61, pp. 143-58.
Pettit, Philip and Smith, Michael (1990) Backgrounding Desire, *Philosophical Review*, 99, pp. 565-92.
Price, Richard (1974) *The Principal Questions of Morals*, D. D. Raphael (ed.) (Oxford: Clarendon Press).
Prichard, H. A. (1928) *Duty and Interest* (Oxford: Clarendon Press).
Railton, Peter (1984) Alienation, Consequentialism, and the Demands of Morality, *Philosophy and Public Affairs*, 13, pp. 134-71.
Ross, W. D. (1930) *The Right and The Good* (New York: Oxford University Press).
Sanford, David H. (1972) Begging the Question, *Analysis*, 32, pp. 197-9.
Sanford, David H. (1981) Superfluous Information, Epistemic Conditions of Inference, and Begging the Question, *Metaphilosophy*, 12, pp. 145-58.
Shafer-Landau, Russ (1998) Moral Judgment and Moral Motivation, *The Philosophical Quarterly*, 48, pp. 353-58.
Shafer-Landau, Russ (1999) Moral Judgment and Normative Reasons, *Analysis*, 59, pp. 33-40.
Smith, Michael (1994) *The Moral Problem* (Oxford: Blackwell).
Smith, Michael (1995) Internal Reasons, *Philosophy and Phenomenological Research*, lv, pp. 109-31.
Smith, Michael (1996a) Internalism's Wheel, in: B. Hooker (ed.) *Truth in Ethics* (Oxford: Blackwell), pp. 69-94.
Smith, Michael (1996b) Reply to Ingmar Persson, *Theoria*, 61, pp. 165-71.
Smith, Michael (1996c) The Argument for Internalism: Reply to Miller, *Analysis*, 56, 175-83.
Smith, Michael (1997) In Defense of The Moral Problem: A Reply to Brink, Copp, and Sayre-McCord, *Ethics*, 108, pp. 84-119.
Smith, Michael (1999) The Non-arbitrariness of Reason: Reply to Lenman, *Utilitas*, 11, pp. 178-93.
Stevenson, Charles L. (1937) The Emotive Meaning of Ethical Terms, *Mind*, 46, pp. 14-31.
Stocker, Michael (1979) Desiring the Bad, *Journal of Philosophy*, 76, pp. 738-53.
Stroud, Barry (1977) *Hume* (London: Routledge & Kegan Paul).
Svavarsdóttir, Sigrún (1999), Moral Cognitivism and Motivation, *Philosophical Review*, 108, pp. 161-219.
Tenenbaum, Sergio (2000) Ethical Internalism and Glaucon's Question, *Noûs*, 34, pp. 108-30.

Watson, Gary (1982) Free Agency, in: G. Watson (ed.) *Free Will* (Oxford: Oxford University Press), pp. 96-110.
Williams, Bernard (1981) Persons, Character and Morality, in: B. Williams, *Moral Luck* (Cambridge: Cambridge University Press), pp. 1-19.

ated.

# NECESSITY, IDENTITY AND TIME

LARS GUNDERSEN

Department of Philosophy
University of Aarhus

## 1. Introduction

It is widely agreed among modal philosophers that there is an intimate connection between necessity and identity. Necessity – or, more precautiously, *de re* necessity – presupposes the idea that one and the same entity can inhabit several qualitatively distinguishable possible scenarios. The claim that water is necessarily $H_2O$, for instance, presupposes the idea that there is a *something*, water, which may obtain in several possible scenarios. To claim that water is necessarily $H_2O$ is to claim that *this* entity has the same molecular structure in all the possible scenarios in which *it* exists. Without the idea of such a transworld self-identical entity, ascriptions to some object of necessary properties become, at best, fallacious – at worst, nonsensical. In this paper I shall argue that there also is an intimate connection between necessity and *time*. In particular, I wish to propose an account of trans-world identity that supervenes on trans-temporal identity.[1]

The potential significance of such an account ought to be obvious. The fact that trans-world identity can be understood in terms of trans-temporal identity effectively takes the sting out of a persistent and influential hostility towards modality: the tendency to refuse *de re* necessity altogether due to its alliance to a 'slum of possibles' and its associated 'breeding ground for disorderly elements' such as trans-world identity relations.[2] I am very much in agreement with the view put forward by Frank Jackson: that declining to take full theoretical advantage of the general possible world framework due to the ontological mysteries raised by that framework "is not that different from refusing to count one's change at the supermarket because of the ontological mysteries raised by numbers".[3] But the present paper will hopefully also provide remedy for those who do not share this view. Although *trans-temporal identity* is by no means an ontologically innocent notion, it is still a notion that we all accept and work with in all sorts of philosophical and practical contexts. If the idea of *de re* necessity can be shown to depend merely on *that* notion rather than on the, for some, anxiety-provoking notion of *trans-world identity*, the way is paved for fully implementing the fertile theoretical, modal tools within *inter alia* philosophy of mind, semantics, philosophy of science and, not least, epistemology – also for those with strong reservations toward ontologically tainted toolboxes.

The idea underlying the present account appears implicitly in several passages of Kripke's canonical work on the matter,[4] such as in his famous dice example where an initial situation, the throwing of some dice A and B, may cause thirty-six different outcomes – or miniature possible worlds – some of which will be qualitatively identical.[5] Here, Kripke tells us, there is no difficulty in identifying die A and die B across the various miniature possible worlds. And why not? The reason, the contention will be, is that in this example die B, for instance, in *each* of the thirty six miniature possible worlds can be traced back to *one and the same* die B from the initial throwing situation. This is so since each of the thirty-six possible B's are trans-temporally identical with that single die B in the initial throwing situation. The suggestion I wish to unfold below is that this line of thought applies to trans-world identity relations on a much larger scale too. In general:

> For any instance of trans-world identity, at any time, t, between several X's – be it persons, poached eggs, rivers or whatever – this trans-world identity supervenes on an initial actual situation, some time t' in the past, in which X exists and which has it that all the various X's-at-t can be traced back to one and the same X-at-t'.

Here is a simple example to illustrate the idea: Consider your own respiration. There are two equal possible near futures. One in which you breathe in before you have finished reading this section and one in which you do not. We can think of this as two possible worlds. One possible world in which you inhale before you have finished reading this section ($w_i$) and one in which you do not ($w_{\sim i}$). And you exist in both worlds!

t is now (*now*) and t' was a few seconds ago. Only you know whether $w_i$ or $w_{\sim i}$ is the actual world. But suppose this world is $w_i$. Now, how is it possible for you to exist both in this world, $w_i$, and in the possible world, $w_{\sim I}$, in which you did not inhale while reading the previous section? You might wish to argue that you only exist in this one world. But you would have a tough time getting that point across. We have, after all, just agreed that you might not have inhaled – that is, that there is a possible scenario in which you did not inhale. If it was not you who did not inhale there, who was it? So, better give in and admit that we have *two* of you: you-here-in-$w_i$ and you-in-$w_{\sim i}$. Both of you are you-at-t. However, a few seconds ago at t' there was only one of you. One you-at-t'.

Presumably, you agree that you-at-t is the very same as you-at-t'. And had this world been $w_{-i}$ you would probably also have agreed that you-at-t is the very same as you-at-t'. So both of you-at-t can be traced back to one and same you-at-t'. And this is how it is possible for you to be in several worlds. At t there were two options open for you regarding your respiration. So, very cleverly, you branched into two, one of which inhaled (you), and one of which did not (you-in-$w_{-i}$). But you are still the same. For both of you are identical with you-at-t', and since identity is both transitive and symmetric, it follows that you and you-in $w_{-i}$ are identical too.

Any instance of trans-world identity is just like that except for the fact that there might be a few more branches to consider. For, as you know, individuals do not branch into two individuals in the same world. So every time someone decides to branch, the whole world and all its additional inhabitants have to be so considerate as to branch with this person such that each of the two branched individuals can get a fully furnished world to live in. Altogether this presents us with an atrocious number of branches.[6]

## 2. Time and Modality

It was only at t' that you-in-$w_i$ started to differ qualitatively from you-in-$w_{-i}$. Before t' both of you were sitting and reading and breathing in the same rhythm. Before t' you shared all your properties with you-in-$w_{-i}$. You were qualitatively identical. And you were numerically identical too. So before the crucial t', all the present account amounts to is a trivial account of trans-world identity in terms of qualitative *and* numerical identity, you being trans-world identical with yourself by virtue of both identical matter and identical qualities.

After t' you and you-in-$w_{-i}$ no longer share all your properties. You were for instance inhaling while other-worldly you was not. So the two of you can no longer be trans-world identical by virtue of qualitative identity. Nor do you share your bodily matter. So you can no longer be identical by virtue of numerical identity. Hence, if you really are the same, which I suggest you are, you must be so by virtue of identical essence. All the present account amounts to after the crucial t' is thus a Kripkean account of trans-world identity in terms of essences.[7]

The crucial new ingredient in the present account is its t'-relative combination of the trivial and the Kripkean account of trans-world identity. This feature also highlights a crucial aspect of modality – an aspect that far too often has been ignored in modal philosophy – namely, *time*. The temporal component in the present account provides the means to deal satisfactorily with many of the objections raised against a pure Kripkean essentialism, objections that many philosophers, including David Lewis, have taken to be decisive against any account of genuine trans-world identity.

The failure to acknowledge the temporal aspect of modality is often reflected grammatically in the fact that possible scenarios are discussed in the present mood as how things possibly *are* rather than in past participle mood as how things *could have been*. In a non-temporal account of modality, the case sketched above, for instance, would be phrased like this: It is possible that you did not inhale shortly after t', for surely there is a possible world somewhere in which you did not thus inhale. But, really, it is not possible that you did not inhale. It *was* a possibility before t'. You *could have* refrained from inhaling, but given that you as a matter of fact inhaled, it is, now, impossible that you acted otherwise. You have passed your chance to change what you did, for time is irreversible.

You might wish to object here that what I just wrote implies that an uncomfortably large number of facts and events are rendered necessary. For it seems to follow that *all* past alternative courses of events have now passed their chance. The *entire* world is thus apparently the way it is with necessity. My response would be that I agree. Only I find it highly *comfortable* that the world necessarily only can be one way.

I hear your objection: in that case it seems to follow that because the world is such a way that for instance this very copy of Danish Yearbook of Philosophy has the spatial position it has, it is *necessary* that this token of Danish Yearbook of Philosophy should have *exactly* that spatial position! Not so. Nothing hinders you – or anyone else for that matter – in moving this token of Danish Yearbook of Philosophy. And if you do so it will change its position. But that is just to say that there are several possible futures *open* for this token of Danish Yearbook of Philosophy with regard to its spatial position.

What? Am I only playing linguistic games here? Linguistic games drawing on the ambiguity of

(1) The world is the way it is

The last bit here – 'the way it is' – can be read either as referring rigidly to the way things as matter of fact have turned out, or it can be read as referring flexibly to whatever, in any hypothetical scenario, satisfies this description. In the former claim I deliberately read it in its flexible sense. Thus read (1) is surely true with necessity. But in the latter claim I deliberately read 'the way it is' in its rigid sense. And thus read (1) is true, but only contingently so. A similar ambiguity crops up in the following example:

(2) Necessarily, Shakespeare was born the year he was

Well, to come clear, in a certain sense I am merely playing games – not solely *linguistic* games, though. For there is a sense in which I believe a proposition such as (2) is true regardless of whether 'the year he was' is read as a flexible or rigid expression. I do not wish to deny outright that now there are other possible worlds – or, as I shall phrase them: possible branches. There are alternative branches, and in some of those Shakespeare was not born in 1564. There are, now, counterfactual branches. And each one of them has its own specific counterfactual past. It is just that these counterfactual branches have 'withered' – they have a different ontological standing than the actual branch and also a different ontological standing than future branches further up in the tree, as it were.

In order to clarify all this I shall now turn to a more formalistic presentation of the central idea. It all sounds, admittedly, a bit metaphysical which may cause some readers to wonder exactly what these metaphysical undertones amount to. Therefore, to begin with I shall present the metaphysical World model preceding and underlying the semantic ideas sketched above.

## 3. The World[8]

The world is everything that is the case. And possible worlds are everything that is the case there. But there are no possible worlds, only the world. And everything that is the case in the world – Caesar lying in his bed in a certain position on his fifth birthday, the cat sitting on the mat, Jones perceiving the cat, your breathing and the sun's burning of hydrogen and oxygen – it is all to be thought of as small temporal Fibres. And some Fibres are very short (Jones perceiving the cat) while others are extremely long (the sun's burning of oxygen and hydrogen). The accretion of all these Fibres is the World. So it is not difficult to conceive of the World as a rope made up of all these Fibres. Now, imagine that we cut a Time-slice, idealized to a temporal thickness of zero, through this rope at a certain time, t. We would thereby cut through a great number of Fibres of various lengths. Let us call such a set of Fibres a Moment.[9] The World thus consists of nothing but Moments.[10] And although Fibres, and thus Moments, have temporal extension we can still associate each Moment with an exact point in time, t, the t, *viz.* where the corresponding Time-slice is cut through the rope. There is therefore no contradiction involved in conceiving of time as dense with Moments, and we shall indeed conceive of time as dense with Moments:

DENSE  $(\forall M_1 M_2) (\exists M_3) (M_1 < M_2) \rightarrow (M_1 < M_3 < M_2))$[11]

So, if $M_1$ is close to $M_2$, (say, $M_2$ is a second from $M_1$) then $M_1$ and $M_2$ will overlap with almost all their constituent Fibres.[12] The $M_1$ Time-slice will intersect with almost the same set of Fibres as the $M_2$ Time-slice. A few Fibres will however end just before $M_2$ and be continued there with a new Fibre. But, because of DENSE, every Fibre belongs to some Moment.

Furthermore, every Moment in the World satisfies transitivity, reflexivity and anti-symmetry:

TRANS  $(\forall M_1 M_2 M_3) ((M_1 < M_2 < M_3) \rightarrow (M_1 < M_3))$
REF  $(\forall M) (M \leq M)$
ANTISYM $(\forall M_1 M_2) ((M_1 < M_2) \rightarrow \neg(M_2 < M_1))$

ANTISYM is more presumptuous than it might appear at first sight. It implies that a third Moment, $M_3$, later than $M_2$, will never be identical to $M_1$, no matter how similar it is to $M_1$. It thus allows for the possibility of permutation-of-era-haecceitism: the idea that two world-states, or eras, can be perfect epistemic counterparts – and yet be distinct. In principle, there are two distinct ways a world state, M, can be represented: Either i) by giving a purely qualitative description of M in a language void of proper names, demonstratives and other rigid designators; call this a Q-representation. Or ii) by giving an account of M in a language including such *de re* vocabulary (as when we say that *this* person does thus and so); call this a K-representation. Permutation-of-era-haecceitism is simply the claim that a K-representation does not supervene on a Q-representation. That is, differences in K-representation do not necessarily imply differences in Q-representation. Or, what comes to the same thing: alternative permutations of K-representations could be qualitatively undetectable. We could have two distinct Moments, qualitatively identical, but only differing in their permutation of individuals. Anti-haecceitism holds that such haecceitistic differences do not make sense. According to anti-haecceitism, every K-representation supervenes on an underlying Q-representation. But this is just what ANTISYM denies: we cannot have an alternative K-permutation of any two world states, $M_1$ and $M_2$, no matter how qualitatively alike they may be.

After all the fuss I made about branching in the previous section, you might expect the next constraint on the ≤-order to concern the flow of the Moments, a constraint which demands that the Moments flow in one riverbed only (there is only *one* World) – but a constraint which still allows the Moments to flow in a branching riverbed; that is to say, a constraint which requires the Moments to flow in *one* riverbed but leaves latitude for a branching Nile-like riverbed. However, such a constraint has disastrous consequences.

Let t' be now (again: *now*). This very Moment – the t'-Moment – may have numerous alternative succeeding Moments. One might be that you continue to read for another half an hour until t. Another one might be that you go to the pub and relax with a pint of Guinness until t. So at t you might either be sitting in a pub enjoying a beer (call this event a b-Fibre) or you might, at t, find yourself sitting and reading (c-Fibre).[13] However, both the b-Fibre and the c-Fibre will be contained in some t-Moments. The b-Fibre-Moment is half an hour after t' and the relevant c-Fibre-Moment is half an hour after t'. So although belonging to distinct alternative futures, those two Moments will still be temporally ordered. They will be simultaneous. And the same point applies to any other two Moments. They will always have a common historical ancestor-Moment some time in the past.[14] And they will both be a certain temporal distance away from this common Moment. And one of the temporal distances will always be either shorter or the same length as the other. So for every two Moments, one of them will always be either before, after or simultaneous with the other. To claim otherwise is just to claim that some alternative future collapses into a time-less vacuum where temporal distances are not measurable at all. And that would be disastrous.

You might wish to object here that although the Moments in each particular alternative future are compatible it may well be that Moments in two alternative futures flow in different directions, as it were, such that Moments from two distinct alternative futures are incompatible. However, it seems to me that Moments, provided that they flow at all, can only flow in two directions: forwards and backwards. I am also convinced that Moments do not flow backwards. But even if they do flow backwards in some alternative 'future', Moments from this future would still be measurable relative to Moments from alternative futures where Moments flow forwards. Hence, all Moments whatsoever are temporally related.[15] That is, Moments do flow in a linear riverbed:

LIN $\quad (\forall M_1 \, M_2) \, ( M_1 \leq M_2 \vee M_2 \leq M_1)$

But the t-b-Fibre (the event that you are drinking beer at t) and the t-c-Fibre (the event that you are still reading at t) are certainly not contained in the same Moment although they are simultaneous. So Moments must, somehow, be ordered in a branching structure. The suggestion is that Moments branch in the following sense:

BRANCH $\quad (\exists M_1 \, M_2) \, ((M_1 \approx M_2) \, \& \, \neg \, (M_1 = M_2)$

This suggestion combined with LIN certainly invites trouble. If every Moment between the t'-Moment and the two t-Moments is temporally related, how do we determine for an arbitrary t''-Moment – t'' being some time between t' and t – whether this t''-Moment belongs to the path of Moments leading to the t-c-Fibre-Moment or to the path of Moments leading to the t-b-Fibre-Moment?

The answer is that due to DENSE every Moment shares some of its Fibres with some succeeding Moment and with some preceding Moment:

PATHforward $\quad (\forall M_1) \, (\exists M_2) \, (\exists F) \, (M_1 < M_2 \, \& \, F \in M_1 \cap M_2)$
PATHbackward $\quad (\forall M_1) \, (\exists M_2) \, (\exists F) \, (M_2 < M_1 \, \& \, F \in M_1 \cap M_2)$[16]

Take any t''-Moment. And take the set of Moments which share some Fibre with a previous Moment which shares some Fibres with a previous Moment which shares some Fibres ... with the t''-Moment. If this set of Moments thus backtracked contains the t-c-Fibre-Moment then the t'' Moment belongs to the t-c-Fibre-Path. If this set of Moments contains the t-b-Fibre-Moment then the t'' Moment belongs to the t-b-Fibre-Path. I shall henceforth refer to the procedure just sketched as 'backtracking'. We could likewise form a chain of Moments by moving forwards along a Path of Fibre-connected Moments ('tracking'). But while the Path constituted by backtracking is unique we can create numerous distinct Paths by tracking.

It still remains to be explained how one and the same Path – such as the path to which the t'-Moment belongs – splits into two distinct paths. LIN and ANTISYM secures that for any Fibre we choose to consider there will be some Moment that is the last Moment to which this Fibre belongs:[17]

SPLIT   $(\forall F) (\exists M_1) ((F \in M_1) \& (\forall M_2) ((M_1 < M_2) \to \neg (F \in M_2)))$

Consider now the t'-c-Fibre again (you sitting and reading at t'). This Fibre had two possible successor-Fibres, a c-Fibre (reading) and a b-Fibre (beer).

This is not to say that the t'-c-Fibre is Y-shaped. Fibres are facts and events. And there is no such event as you drinking beer in a pub and reading in your office at the same time. The t'-c-Fibre ends, and where it ends, two possible successor-Fibres begin.

Our assumption is that there is only one Path at t'. SPLIT now allows for two simultaneous $M_2$'s, each containing a Fibre distinct from yet succeeding some particular $M_1$-Fibre. In particular, with our t'-Moment substituted for $M_1$ we get, as the two simultaneous $M_2$'s, a t-b-Fibre-Moment and a t-c-Fibre-Moment. These two Moments belong to different Paths. But by backtracking they can both be subsumed under the same (forking) Path as our original t'-c-Fibre-Moment.

Let us call the union of the two sets formed by backtracking from a given M and tracking forward from the same M an 'M-Branch'. As mentioned above, we can only form one unique Branch by backtracking, but we can form numerous distinct Branches by tracking, so there are numerous distinct M-Branches. Let us call a maximal set of such M-branches the 'M-Tree'. We have now succeeded in conceptualising a branching World although within the framework of linear time: the World is nothing but a big Tree. Each particular M-Tree converges with other M-trees as we backtrack downwards along the Trunk. And the (idealised) Moment, $M_0$, at the very bottom of this Trunk, is the point where all the Trees converge. The World is the maximal set consisting of each of these converging M-trees: the $M_0$-tree.

There are two theoretical advantages associated with the Tree-metaphor. Firstly, it suggests that the alternative futures – i.e., the Branches further up in the tree – really do exist and that they are all metaphysically on a par. There is no such thing as *one* metaphysically privileged Branch: *the* actual future – a future that we, with our limited cognitive resources, are not capable of predicting yet; but a future that is nevertheless predestined as the way the World is going to be.

The other theoretical advantage associated with the Tree-metaphor is its implicit suggestion that the future Branches, although already existing now, may not yet be full-grown. It is often assumed in metaphysical disputes about the future that there is a sharp distinction between realism and anti-realism. A semantic argument for anti-realism about the future, for instance, has it that *every* future-tensed proposition is in principle verification-transcendent and, hence, could be neither acquired nor manifested if comprehending it consists in knowledge of its truth condition. But, in fact, *some* fractions of the future do exist. No one really believes this is the last existing Moment. You certainly do not: there is no way you would spend your very last moment reading this paper – more likely would you be sitting in a pub enjoying your last pint of Guinness. There *is* a Moment succeeding the present Moment, and after that one there is another one, and after that one yet another one, and so on. And so on *ad infinitum*? *That* is the philosophically interesting question.[18] The Tree picture offers one answer: that in a sense there exists another Moment and so on *ad infinitum*: the branches are continuously growing. In another sense there is no next Moment and so on *ad infinitum*: the branches do not (yet) grow into heaven.

There are also two potentially misleading features of the Tree metaphor. First, the trunk of a tree is always distinctively thicker than any of its branches. This might seduce us to think that the Branches run parallel – and thus constitute a fat Trunk – while they are qualitatively identical and then split into thinner Branches as they diverge qualitatively. However, the Branches that constitute the Trunk in our World model are not only qualitatively identical, but they are also numerically identical. They do not run parallel; they converge in one *common* Trunk:[19]

ONETRUNK $(\forall M_1 M_2) (\exists M_3) (M_1\text{-tree} \cup M_2\text{-tree} \subseteq M_3\text{-tree})$

Secondly, and much worse, the Tree metaphor might seduce us to think that the one Trunk diverges downwards into a network of Roots. It does not. Whereas for each particular Moment there is a multitude of possible future Branches, there is only one past Branch. The past is unique:

NOROOTS
$(\forall M_1 M_2 M_3) ((\{M_1, M_2\} \subseteq M_3\text{-tree} \ \& \ M_1 \notin M_2\text{-tree}) \rightarrow (M_3 \leq M_1))$[20]

So if $M_0$ is the very first Moment, the World is just an $M_0$-tree. But I prefer to remain agnostic as to whether there is such a very first Moment.

Did I cheat? First I defined Fibres in terms of something fairly well known, namely, facts and events in the world, and then I defined Moments in terms of Fibres, Branches in terms of Moments, and finally Trees in terms of Branches. Now I claim that the World is something less familiar, namely, a Tree! Well, perhaps I did cheat a little bit. But I believe you know exactly what I mean by World, Fibre, Moment, Branch and Tree, although these notions are only inter-definable. The World model is introduced with a view to depicting the ontological structure of the world in a clear and systematic way. In the following section I shall explore the corresponding semantic findings – in particular I shall examine and defend the advertised semantic relations between trans-world and trans-temporal identity relations. Even if we are miles apart regarding the ontological intuitions driving the World model, we might still find some agreement in the semantic consequences I shall draw from the World-model.

## 4. Semantics of Trans-world Identicals, Tenses and Modalities

I mentioned above that the driving thought in the present account is that modality is intimately related with temporality. It would be nice if this relation were a simple one. It would be nice, for instance, if the accessibility relations adhered to in possible world frameworks could simply be considered the temporal relation between Moments in our World model. All we would have to do, then, would be to investigate which modal system is characterised by the class of all linear, dense, transitive, reflexive and anti-symmetrical $[M, \leq]$-models.[21] Diodorian modality is a good example of such a simple relation between modality and time. Diodorian modality is characterised by the linear, transitive, reflexive and anti-symmetrical $[M, \leq]$ models.[22] And the corresponding system is **S 4.3**.[23] The main intuition underlying Diodorian modality is thus an understanding of possibility as 'it is or will be the case; and an understanding of necessity as 'it is the case and will always be the case'.

Diodorian modality is however also a good example of a theory that fails to provide an adequate picture of what modality is. The vexing challenge with modality is exactly that, to a great extent, it is about what never is the case – but, nonetheless, *could* have been the case. An amended characterising model that replaces temporal linearity with temporal branching does to some extent account for this feature of modality. According to such a model possibility is understood as 'it is the case now or will be the case in some alternative future'. But the problem with such a suggestion is that every possible future would still in some sense be relative to the present. Take poor Fred, for instance. He lost both legs in the Second World War. There is no possible future in which he will go jogging every morning. So, according to the amended Diodorian theory, it is impossible that Fred goes jogging every morning. But surely this is not impossible. Things could have gone otherwise in the Second World War.

I believe there is a close relation between time and modality. Not one as simple, however, as is suggested by a Diodorian theory. That the present account is more sophisticated than Diodorian theory in that respect is reflected in the fact that the World model encompasses *both* purely temporal features (DENSE, TRANS, REF, ANTISYM and LIN), *and* modal characteristics (SPLIT, ONETRUNK and NOROOTS).[24] This complexity allows for a much richer expressibility in the corresponding semantics. In particular it allows for both temporal and modal relata, neither of which collapses into the other. It allows, for instance, for descriptions of modal, although simultaneous, states of affairs (such as Fred possibly going jogging now). It is great to have a semantics that allows for temporal descriptions; it is also great to have a semantics that allows for modal descriptions, but a semantics that allows for both without putting limitations on either is a sheer joy. Only thus can we describe reality in an authentic manner – intermingled in both temporal and modal patterns as it is. Granted such a two-dimensional semantics we can, for instance, give expression to the plausible idea that other-worldly you is the same as this-worldly you due to a common temporal ancestor.

Let us now proceed to work out the exact semantics for this latter idea. The suggestion is that trans-world identity relations can be worked out along the following lines:

$X$-in-$M_1$ $=_w$ $Y$-in-$M_2$ $\leftrightarrow$
$(\exists M_3)$ $(\exists Z)$ ($Z$-in-$M_3$ & $\{M_1, M_2\} \subseteq M_3$-tree & $Z$-in-$M_3 =_t X$-in-$M_1$ & $Z$-in-$M_3 =_t Y$-in-$M_2$)[25]

Roughly, the suggestion is that two other-worldly entities, X and Y (the $M_1$ and $M_2$ moments being Moments from two distinct Branches), are trans-world identical if there is some entity Z in some common ancestor Moment $M_3$ such that Z is trans-temporally identical to both X and Y. The constraint that $M_3$ is a common ancestor Moment to $M_1$ and $M_2$ is expressed by the first conjunct clause on the right-hand side: that $M_1$ and $M_2$, although belonging to distinct Branches, still belong to the same $M_3$-Tree – that is to say, $M_3$ is the converging point for the $M_1$- and $M_2$-Branches.

Usually it is highly suspicious when a semantic theory attributes semantic values to a given formulae in terms of more complex formulas. In this case it seems that the semantics of an identity expression is determined in terms of two other identity statements. But things are not as bad as one might fear. The left-hand-side identity sign is, as mentioned, a trans-world identity sign, whereas the two right-hand-side identity signs are constrained to identity within one branch, that is, to trans-temporal identity. This is, as mentioned, secured by the clause that $\{M_1, M_2\} \subseteq M_3$-tree. By ONETRUNK and the definition of M-trees it follows that $(\exists B_1) (\{M_1, M_3\} \subseteq B_1) \& (\exists B_2) (\{M_2, M_3\} \subseteq B_2)$. The present account thus in effect states that criteria for trans-world identity can generally be given in terms of criteria for trans-temporal identity. That is to say, provided an adequate semantics for trans-temporal identity statements can be worked out, we have not only provided a metaphysical account of how it is possible for one and the same object to exist in several worlds, we have also – as a bi-product – solved the analogous epistemological problem: how it is possible to *identify* a given object in other-worldly surroundings.

But this is not all. There are also independent reasons for believing in the present account of identity and necessity. We shall focus on just one semantical aspect that, alone, proves the worth of the present account. Consider the two sentences:

> (3) This token of Danish Yearbook of Philosophy could have been on Bali Island now, and
>
> (4) It is possible for this token of Danish Yearbook of Philosophy to be at Bali Island now

(3) is trivially true. If any property is contingent, the one attributed in (3) is. To be situated a particular place at a particular time is, if anything, something that could have gone differently. (4), on the other hand, is trivially false. Things could have gone otherwise. But they went in only one of these ways. In particular, things went in such a way that this token of Danish Yearbook of Philosophy happens to be right *here*. (I sincerely hope you are not sitting on a beach on Bali Island while reading this). It is thus not a possibility now for this token of Danish Yearbook of Philosophy to be anywhere else besides right here.

Note that the ambiguity between (3) and (4) is not a classical *de re, de dicto* ambiguity. In order to see the contrast, consider the following:

> (5) It is a possibility for a square token of Danish Yearbook of Philosophy to be triangular

(5) too is ambiguous. But the ambiguity in (5) draws on whether the description 'a square token of Danish Yearbook of Philosophy' is read as a rigid or flexible designator. In classical modal semantics, this ambiguity can be accounted for by attributing either wide or narrow scope to the modal operator relative to the scope of the description. But both (3) and (4) are about *this* token of Danish Yearbook of Philosophy. The ambiguity here is thus of a different kind and cannot be resolved by scope considerations – and, to the best of my knowledge, not by any other means either. Let us call the ambiguity featured in (3) and (4) 'now-ambiguity'. I take it to be a great advantage of the semantics founded on the World model that it can actually account satisfactorily for such now-ambiguities.

It seems that now-ambiguities somehow draw on differences in attribution of scope to the 'now'-operator. It can quantify over the whole modal statement and indicate that it is true now, or it can quantify over the embedded statement only. Let the embedded sentence A be "this token of Danish Yearbook of Philosophy is on Bali Island". This gives the following two scope interpretations of the now-operator:

> (6) Now ($\lozenge$ A), or
>
> (7) $\lozenge$ Now (A)[26]

It is notworthy that in non-temporal Kripke semantics, these two scope attributions will never cause any difference in the semantic evaluation. For, in a Kripkean view, (7) is true if and only if there – somewhere in a Kripke model – is a possible world which, right now, has it that A. But such a model would, automatically, also satisfy (6). For in that case there would, now, be a possible world in which A. And, the other way round, if there, now, is a possible world in which A, then there is also a possible world that – right now – has it that A.

Not so in the present view. In the present account the 'now' in (6) only concerns the Moment of utterance ($M_u$). It indicates that the Moment of utterance is the present Moment (now-M). So (6) is true if $V(\lozenge A, \text{now-M}) = T$. The 'now' in (7), on the other hand, indicates that there is a Moment, *simultaneous* with $M_u$, that contains an A-Fibre; that is, it suggests that not only is there an A-Fibre in the World ($V(\lozenge A, M_c) = T$), but furthermore there is an A-Fibre that is contained in a Moment simultaneous with $M_c$ ( $(\exists M) (M \approx M_c$ & A-Fibre $\in M)$.

(6) and (7) are obviously not semantically equivalent. $V(6) = T$. For, surely there is some A-Fibre in the World (A being the fact that this token of Danish Yearbook of Philosophy is on Bali Island). But what about $V(7)$? You might feel inclined to say that although it is not quite as obvious that there is an A-fibre contained in a *simultaneous* Moment, it is definitely not impossible either. So $V(7)$ could be T too. This is correct. But as long as $V(7)$ could be F, this is sufficient to highlight the difference in semantic content between (6) and (7).

We can elucidate this semantic difference by choosing "The now-Moment has come true" as (B1), and "this token of Danish Yearbook of Philosophy is on Bali Island" as (B2)". Now let B be a conjunction of B1 and B2. Now let us consider the following:

(8) Now ($\lozenge$B), and

(9) $\lozenge$ now (B)

$V(8)$ is still T. For surely there is a Moment, M, somewhere in the World that has it that both B1 and B2: In order to satisfy B1, M must have it that now-M actually has come true, that is $M \in$ now-M-Branch & now-M $\leq$ M. To satisfy B2, M must contain a B2-Fibre (B2-Fibre $\in$ M). To satisfy both B1 and B2 it must be the case that ($\exists$ now-M-Branch) ($\exists$ M) (M $\in$ now- Moment-Branch & now-Moment $\leq$ M & B2-Fibre $\in$ M). All (8) amounts to is thus the claim that it might be that this token of Danish Yearbook of Philosophy will find its way to Bali Island some time in the future. And surely there is a possible future that holds just that. So $V(8) = T$.

(9), on the other hand, claims that there is a *simultaneous* Moment, M', that satisfies both B1 and B2. To satisfy B1, M' must have it that now-M actually has come true, that is, M' $\in$ now-M-Branch & now-M $\leq$ M'. But given that M' is simultaneous with now-Moment, this can only be so if M' $\approx$ now-Moment. But to satisfy B2, M' must contain a B2-Fibre (B2-Fibre $\in$ M'). (9) is thus tantamount to the claim not merely that there is a possible future in which this token of Danish Yearbook of Philosophy has found its way to Bali Island but, additionally, that this possible future has been *instantiated*. But whereas the first conjunct, as we have just seen, is satisfied, the second surely is not. So V (9) = F. In general: narrow scope interpretations of the now-operator imply wide scope interpretations: ◊ now (P) → Now (◊P), but not *vice versa*.[27]

Implicit in all this is the idea that instantiation is a dynamic process. This is what I had in mind when talking about 'withered' branches. In a certain sense every Branch has the same ontological status. Every future branch exists mind-independently as non-instantiated *possibililia*. Metaphorically, we can say that a branch becomes instantiated by a nutrient sap that moves upwards (and only upwards) in the Tree – a sap that can only nourish one Branch. The other non-nourished Branches wither continuously. So in this sense there is an asymmetry among the *past* Branches, as only one of them is alive. But the withered Branches do not fall off; they remain on the Tree as monuments to how things could have gone.

## 5. Conclusion

The account of necessity, identity and time I have been developing insists on both temporal and modal notions as basic and irreducible. The main idea is that all trans-world identical entities are trans-temporally identical with a common temporal ancestor. And it is by virtue of this common ancestor that it is possible to establish the necessary trans-world criteria of identity. With such a trans-world identity criterion it is possible to develop a satisfactory semantics for trans-world identity statements in terms of trans-temporal identity. The model for such a semantics was developed in the World model. It was demonstrated how this model proves its theoretical worth in dealing satisfactorily with some of the semantic aspects of now-ambiguities – aspects that cannot be accounted for by a traditional Kripke model. In the World model such ambiguities can be explained by drawing on different scope attributions to the ◊-operator in expressions of the form: 'now P but possibly now not P'. It is thus an ambiguity distinct from the traditional *de re, de dicto* ambiguity, which draws on different scope attributions to definite descriptions. Although the ideas laid out in the World model have only been tested on two particular semantic problems, the problems of trans-world identity and now-ambiguities, it will most likely prove its theoretical usefulness in dealing with other semantic puzzles accruing from messy complexities of intermingled modal and temporal *relata*.[28]

## Notes

1. This paper is a follow-up paper to a previous paper on trans-world identity published in Danish Yearbook of Philosophy, vol **30** (1995).
2. The *locus classicus* is Quine 1948. Here Quine, notoriously, illustrates his point with the rhetorical question whether the fat possible man in the doorway is the same as the fat and bald possible man in the doorway. See also Quine 1961.
3. Jackson 1998, p. 11.
4. Kripke 1972
5. Ibid., p. 21.
6. For reasons spelled out in McCall 1994, pp. 94-114, we actually have non-denumerably infinitely many if we take the Theory of Relativity into consideration. And even within a Newtonian world-picture, we have (denumerably) infinitely many branches.
7. For a critical discussion of this Kripkean account, see Gundersen 1995.
8. This section draws heavily on the following works: Prior [1967], Thomason [1970], van Benthem [1983] & [1988] Belnap [1994], Belnap & Green [1994], McCall [1994] and Oehrstoem & Hasle [1994]. The present World model is original.
9. Sometimes I shall index my Moments with a time (t-Moments) or a content (x-Fibre-Moments) or both (t-x-Fibre-Moments).
10. Everyone who has played Pictionary will know how difficult it is to picture, for instance, 'Jones is perceiving a cat'. This is easy, however, compared to the challenge it is actually to isolate the Fibre that Jones is conceiving a cat from the multitude of remaining Fibres in the World. One reason is that this Fibre is interwoven with the Fibres that Jones is courageous, a man, has four children, is fond of dogs, and so on and so forth. The mutual relationship between World Fibres is thus far more complex than is usually the case for fibres in a rope. Despite this intermingling, I see no reason why it should be impossible, in principle, to carve out each particular Fibre of the World. The underlying claim here is, I suppose, that each fibre is spatially complete.
11. Terminology: The Ms are Moments. '<' is the temporal B-series operator, where M1 < M2 means that M1 is before M2. I shall also make use of the following operators: '≈' which is simultaneity. ' ≤', where M1 ≤ M2 means M1 < M2 or M1 ≈ M2. And, finally, '=' which is identity (not to be confused with simultaneity).

    For convenience, I shall sometimes use '<' and sometimes '≤' when laying down the various temporal constraints on my model. When it comes to characterising the temporal modal logic I am after in terms of frames, it will however be most advantageous to conceive of my model as a ≤-ordering.
12. To say that the World is the totality of Moments implies that we get a World containing a large number of repetitious Fibres. A more precise statement would be: Let { $F_n$ : n ∈ ω} be an enumeration of every Fibre, F. Let $\Gamma^0$ be $F_1$. And let $\Gamma^{n+1} = \Gamma^n ~^U \{F_n\}$ if $F_n \notin . \Gamma^n$; otherwise $\Gamma^{n+1} = \Gamma^n$. Finally, let $\Gamma^\infty = ~^U_{n \in \omega}. \Gamma^n$. Then the World = $\Gamma^\infty$.
13. And c-Fibres here have nothing whatsoever to do with c-Fibre stimulation!
14. Unless there are several Worlds; In other words, unless some Moments are spatially and temporally disconnected from this very Moment. This, however, is an incredible idea (for reasons spelled out in Gundersen (1995)). In the present essay I shall thus take the liberty to bracket that possibility.
15. In a sense this is fairly uninteresting, the sense, namely, in which it merely amounts to the claim that time is absolute. And worse: in the same sense is it blatantly false – science has proved that time is not absolute but relative. But as long as it is presupposed that each of the alternative t-Moments is governed by non-accelerating space-time matrices, there is still a sense

in which it reflects an insight. And even if this Newtonian presupposition is not satisfied, there is still a sense in which the theses that all Moments are comparable at least is true: All Moments are comparable relative to a given space-time matrix in one of the alternative futures. And as only one alternative future will be instantiated, this means that all Moments are comparable, absolutely, to this space-time matrix.
16. 'F' being short for Fibre.
17. Because of LIN, all Moments containing the Fibre will be temporally ordered, and because of ANTISYM, they will be uniquely ordered.
18. Wright expresses the same point in Wright [1991], where he defends anti-realism about the future *but* subsumes 'the near future' under the present. His metaphor for this view is a moving train. Everything that can be seen from the carriage window is 'the present' and whatever is beyond the horizon is 'the future'. In Wright's view new 'presents' come into being as the train moves forward and new landscapes become visible. Likewise, in my view the new futures come into being as we gradually move upwards in the M0-tree. The crucial difference between the two views is that I admit for realism far beyond the 'visible' near future.
19. In Lewis 1986 terminology: branching versus divergence.
20. NOROOTS of course also provides an assurance against downwards convergence further above in the Tree.
21. I.e., is sound and complete relative to these models.
22. For a detailed account of alternative characterising models for **S4.3**, see Hughes & Cresswell (1984) pp. 81-6.
23. S4 with the additional axiom L(LA → B) v L(LB → A).
24. To be sure, there is, still, only one World. When I henceforth refer to other worlds and worldly relations, I really mean other branches and branch relations.
25. Terminology: '=w' for trans-world identity and '=t' for trans-temporal identity.
26. A third possibility is that 'now' quantifies over the predicate only – ◊ (This token of Danish Yearbook of Philosophy now (is on Bali Island) ) – but I cannot see any sense in which this interpretation should differ from (6).
27. I have elaborated further upon semantics based on the World model in general and now-ambiguities in particular in Gundersen (1997).
28. Thanks to Paul Castell, Bob Hale, Stephen Read and Michael Redhead for helpful comments.

# References

Belnap, N.: 'Agents in Branching Time', in Copeland (1994).
Bentham, J.: *The Logic of Time*. Dordrect, 1983.
Dummett, M.: 'Bringing About the Past', in Dummett (1978).
'The Reality of the Past', in Dummett (1978).
'A Defense of McTaggart's Proof of the Unreality of Time', in Dummett (1978).
Gundersen, L.: 'On Now-Ambiguities', in *Perspectives on Time*, Faye (red.) *Boston Studies in Philosophy of Science* (1997).
Hughes & Cresswell: *An Introduction to Modal Logic*, Methuen, 1968.
Jackson, F.: *From Metaphysics to Ethics*. Oxford: Oxford University Press, 1998.
Kaplan, D.: 'Trans-world Heir Lines', in Loux (1979).
'How to Russel a Frege-Church', in Loux (1979).
Kripke, S.A.: 'A Comleteness Theorem for Modal Logic', in *Symbolic Logic*, 1953.
'Semantical Considerations on Modal Logic', in *Acta Philosophica Fennic,*1963.
'Identity and Necessity', in *Identity and Necessity* (Munitz ed.), 1971.

|  |  |
|---|---|
|  | 'Speaker's Reference and Semantic reference', in *Contemporary Perspectives in Philosophy of Language*. French, Howard &Uehling (eds.). Minnesota, 1979. |
|  | *Naming and Necessity.* Blackwell, 1972. |
| Lewis, D.: | 'Counterpart Theory and Quantified Modal Logic', in Loux [1979]. |
|  | *Counterfactuals.* Harvard, 1973. |
|  | *On the Plurality of Worlds.* Blackwell, 1986. |
|  | *Names and Descriptions.* Chicago. |
| Loux (ed.): | *The Possible and the Actual.* Cornell, 1979. |
| McCall, S.: | *A Model of the Universe.* Oxford, 1994. |
| Plantinga, A.: | 'Trans-world Identity or Worldbound Individuals', in Loux (1979). |
|  | *The Nature of Necessity.* Oxford, 1984. |
| Prior, A.: | *Past, Present and Future. Oxford*, 1967. |
| Prior, A. & Fine, K.: | *Worlds, Times and Selves.* Duckworth, 1977. |
| Quine, O.: | 'On What There Is', *Review of Metaphysics.* 1948. |
|  | *From a Logical Point of View.* Harvard, 1961. |
| Salmon, U.: | 'The Logic of What Might Have Been', *Philosophical Review*, 1989. |
| Stalnaker, R.: | 'Possible Worlds', in Loux [1979] |
| Thomason: | 'Indeterminism and Truth Value Gaps', in *Theoria*, 1974. |
| Williams, C.: | *Being, Identity and Truth.* Oxford, 1992. |
| Williamson, T.: | *Identity and Discrimination.* Blackwell, 1991. |
| Wright, C.: | *Realism, Meaning and Truth.* Blackwell, 1991. |
|  | 'Eternal Truths, True Value Links and *Nineteen Eighty Four'*, in Wright (1991). |
| Øhrstrøm, P. & Hasle, P.: | *Tense Logic – From Ancient Ideas to Artificial Intelligence.* Kluwer, 1995. |

# LIBERALISM, NEUTRALITY, AND CIVIL SOCIETY[1]

MORTEN EBBE JUUL NIELSEN

Department of Education, Philosophy and Rhetoric
University of Copenhagen

## I. Introduction

It is well known that most strands of modern philosophical liberalism advocate one or another version of state neutrality. In this essay, I want to show the inadequacy of a strategy invoked by some liberal theorists to preserve a certain kind of state neutrality, namely neutrality of justification. Some liberals argue that the neutrality of justification is compatible with a range of state activities, including, for example, sponsorship for the arts. However, I shall try to show that such activities violate the principle of justificatory neutrality. This is the main purpose of the article. But the argument is not intended to imply that neutrality must disappear altogether from the overall liberal framework. Therefore, I will also sketch an alternative, less demanding, but more workable idea of neutrality fully compatible with state actions in areas where contemporary neutralist liberalism cannot operate without grave difficulties.

Discussion will proceed as follows. First, I will present and analyse the main features of standard formulations of neutrality of justification. Special attention here will be paid to the link between liberal state neutrality and the distinction between the right and the good (II-IV). Second, I will outline an alternative version of neutrality (V). Third, I will sketch an argument designed to show that a liberal state must in some circumstances take action in order to maintain liberal culture, and that this liberal culture is a necessary condition of a liberal state (VI). Fourth, I will elaborate the liberal strategy to maintain neutrality mentioned above, and show that it fails (VII). Fifth, and lastly, I will discuss some of the implications of this last failing (VIII).

## II. The problem of neutrality

Let us define neutrality of justification thus: *a state is neutral iff it does not (or cannot) justify its actions with reference to any conceptions of the good.* What in this context should be understood by 'conceptions of the good' will be discussed below, but for now it suffices to characterise the term as applying to any broad, qualitative outlook on what constitutes the good life. For example, an ascetic, vegetarian ideal of the good life could count as a conception of the good.

One problem for the theorist who wants to argue for the desirability and viability of a such a neutral state is this: if the state is neutral, state action in areas where substantial[2] policies are connected with conceptions of the good seems to be impossible, or at least very limited. However, if such action is ruled out, the areas of justifiable activity for the state are drastically reduced. One wants to ask, for instance: what kind of education policies could be genuinely neutral? How could a neutral state give any kind of support to the arts? Could the state operate a genuinely just, but truly neutral health care policy?[3]

One strategy for maintaining state neutrality without reducing the legitimate sphere of state action to an absolute minimum runs as follows. State neutrality would be preserved if the state could act "in" the different areas where substantial policies are connected with conceptions of the good, but still leaves the *evaluation* of differing conceptions of the good to lie outside the apparatus of the state. If this were so, the state would act, not as an arbiter, but merely as an allegedly neutral distributor of means. Any inevitably good-oriented evaluation would take place in *civil society* – that is, in the more or less formalised structure of free association among free citizens within the framework of state *law*, but outside the sphere of state *justification* and *coercion*. The state would not get dirty hands.

The question is whether this proposal to maintain neutrality whilst allowing the state to work in areas intimately connected with conceptions of the good is a viable one. The answer, I shall argue, is that it is not. Civil society, however conceived, cannot serve as a good-oriented evaluating forum for the state in this way without fatally compromising state neutrality.

### III. Standard Versions of State Neutrality and the Distinction Between the Right and the Good

Joseph Raz argues that there are two distinct, but closely interrelated notions of state neutrality.[4] "Neutral political concern" is the idea that the state must aim to help or hinder different life-plans of the citizens to an equal degree.[5] With Kymlicka, we can safely subsume this under the heading "neutrality of consequences". It is the other notion, "the exclusion of ideals", that involves the idea that government is not to justify its actions with reference to conceptions of the good. This is what we have been referring to as the neutrality of justification.

State neutrality is often described as one of the cornerstones of modern mainstream liberal thought. Rawls' *A Theory of Justice* unsurprisingly provides a prime example. Leaving subtle complexities of interpretation aside,[6] Rawls argues that we should picture ourselves as hypothetical rational agents in an initial situation of choice. In this situation we are behind a "veil of ignorance" which renders our personal conceptions of the good unknowable. Thus purified of our idiosyncrasies, we would come to choose – or find – a basic structure of society that accords with principles determining what is *right*. This leaves room for actual individuals to pursue their personal ideas of the *good* (i.e. their particular religious, philosophical, and 'spiritual' ideas, and a vast range of personal affections, tastes and desires).[7] However, the state should not act on, or enforce, policies based on conceptions of the good.[8]

The soundness and cogency of Rawls' distinction between the good and the right has come under much scrutiny. It is indeed deemed fraudulent by many so-called communitarians.[9] In philosophical critiques of liberal neutrality it is often claimed that there is an intrinsic connection between liberal neutrality, on the one hand, and the distinction between the right and the good, on the other; and that the former fails because of the unsoundness of the latter. A number of reasons for doubting the soundness of the distinction have been offered. However, for the present purposes I shall not examine the cogency of the distinction any further. I can push through my argument without rejecting or confirming it.

One might nevertheless wonder whether limits to the legitimate areas of state action stem from, and are reinforced by, the insistence on the very distinction itself. For the concept of the right, as used by Rawls in *A Theory of Justice*, is formal, universal, and procedural. By contrast, the concept of the good is substantive, particular and subjective. If I understand him correctly, Rawls believes that the concept of the right could be used to rule that the pieces of a given cake should be distributed equally among recipients, unless an unequal distribution favours the worst off. To find out what *kind* of cake should be distributed, we would have to invoke conceptions of the good. (We can speak of a 'good cake', but hardly of a 'just cake'.) Similarly, the concept of the right *might* tell us that some basic level of education must be open to all members of society, but I fail to see how we can determine what *kind* of education should be provided without invoking a conception of the good. Indeed I doubt whether a valid argument in favour of providing everyone with a basic level of education can be made without a discussion of what constitutes *good* education, i.e. in the absence of a conception of the good. But that is beyond the limits of this essay.

And anyhow, the matter I wish to discuss from now on does not rely on the distinction between the right and the good (or on the falsehood thereof). The notion of state neutrality does not in my view necessarily presuppose that "the right is prior to the good." Although it is often found in a deontological framework, I think that we can look at state neutrality in itself without invoking the concepts of the right and the good.

## IV. Clarifications of Neutrality

To avoid confusion about the very idea of neutrality, we need to make some clarificatory remarks: first, the concept of neutrality does not necessarily apply to the process of *actual deliberation*. It does not matter whether the real political process appeals to conceptions of the good. In almost all cases, political arguments will evolve around different conceptions of the good life, especially in a democratic context. However, this misses the point. Ultimately, what matters is that a given policy could either be given a neutralist justification or shown to have neutral consequences – and this is independent of the question whether the deliberation leading to the policy actually followed some neutralist scheme (of deliberation).

More importantly, if taken at face value, the formulation of state neutrality ("*a state is neutral iff it does not (or cannot) justify its actions with reference to any conceptions of the good*") seems to imply that the state can take no action whatsoever: any coercive act[10] of the government's can be interpreted as an endorsement of a particular way of life, and any action of the state can be seen as having non-neutral consequences.[11] It might seem, then, that the neutral state cannot make laws outlawing murder, because in doing so it would favour the way of life of the non-murderer over that of the murderer. No such absurd conclusion follows, however, because the government's adoption of such a prohibition can be grounded in an appeal to the rights-based idea of protection of life and a right to live, or so the liberal would argue. This appeal need involve no commitments vis-à-vis the good-based idea – unavailable to the neutralist – that a life without murder is better than a life with murder.[12]

Do these clarifications rule out discussion of so-called *consequential* neutrality? Do they exclude the kind of neutrality Raz calls "neutral political concern"? It seems that they do. Kymlicka has argued that, even though some formulations in Rawls' work can be read as endorsements of consequential neutrality, there are strong reasons for thinking that he does not occupy this position. For one thing, the respect for civil liberties – for freedom of speech and association – that is so essential both for Rawls and in liberalism generally will create a marketplace of ideas where "…satisfying and valuable ways of life will tend to drive out those which are worthless and unsatisfying."[13] Secondly, the egalitarian strand in Rawls' thought – the idea of equality of resources or "primary goods" that lies at the heart of his thinking – will penalise expensive ways of life and favour more modest ways of life. In other words, people should be held responsible for their choices of life-style.[14] Taken together, these two points strongly suggest that Rawls[15] endorses neutrality of justification, not neutrality of consequences. The implementation of Rawlsian policies would have non-neutral consequences. This fits in nicely with the conclusion Simon Caney draws from his analysis of consequentialist defences of neutrality, namely: "Now neutralists *invariably* defend justificatory neutrality and eschew the two consequentialist conceptions of neutrality. This is important because critics of neutrality often foist consequential accounts of neutrality on neutralists and then argue (plausibly) that such neutrality is unattainable."[16] Thus, even though neutrality of consequences is a theoretical option, we should interpret Rawls' work, and modern deontological liberalism generally, as advocating justificatory, not consequentialist, neutrality.

### V. A Further Notion of Neutrality: Neutrality as Fairness

The two concepts mentioned so far have traditionally been treated as the whole story about state neutrality: such neutrality is either neutrality of consequences or neutrality of justification. At this point I want to suggest, however, that there is another, more encompassing, but less demanding, notion of neutrality at play in most, if not all, liberal thought. I call this *neutrality as fairness*.[17]

Neutrality as fairness consists of two claims. (1) Our common sense notion of a neutral state is something like this: it is a state that does not *arbitrarily* favour or hinder defined categories of individual (e.g. by proclaiming that everyone named Jones must pay 5% more in tax, or that any bald person is entitled to a free scholarship); ways of life (e.g. by favouring the practice of eating asparagus over the practice of eating carrots where no independent reason could be given for such a policy); and so on.

Naturally, this is an almost vacuous definition. It could be endorsed consistently with any political theory that takes it as a *conditio sine qua non* that *valid independent reasons* must be given for any legitimate political action (including issuing laws, and the like). But it is not a *wholly* vacuous definition. It excludes a) any 'pre-modern' political thinking that does not count the provision of *independent* reasons as a necessary condition of legitimacy; b) sceptical theories of Realpolitik that equate legitimacy with power; and c) theories that fetishise democracy by positing a (mysterious) internal connection between what the majority decides on one hand and legitimacy on the other.[18]

The second claim places neutrality as fairness in a liberal context. (2) Neutrality as fairness involves the claim that *individual autonomy* (the protection and furthering thereof) is among the proper aims of political actions and institutions. Fair and neutral treatment entails treating individuals *as* individuals: holding individuals responsible for their individual actions, without taking such things as race, class and gender into consideration. Similarly, political actions are justified only because they benefit (protect, or further the interest of) *individuals*; it would run counter to the idea of fairness if someone were to benefit or suffer *because*, say, they belonged to a certain race or class.

To sum up, then, neutrality as fairness expresses two common, and distinctly modern, intuitions: that state activity must be backed by valid grounds, and that the individual is both a *worthy participant* in the political process and *a responsible agent* whose autonomy is prima facie inviolable, and (intrinsically or extrinsically) valuable.

Note that this concept of neutrality as fairness does not entail the specific idea of neutrality of justification: it only rules out the arbitrary, that is, *unjustifiable*, favouring or penalising of individuals. If a conception of the good life is both *true* and compatible with the autonomy of other citizens – citizens with conflicting conceptions of the good life, perhaps – then the state can justify its actions by appealing to that conception of the good life.

I will later return to this broader notion of neutrality, but for now I want to ask why the neutrality of justification narrows the area of legitimate state action to much; why the state should be concerned with the citizen's conceptions of the good; and why it would want to take action in the cultural marketplace[19] in the first place.

## VI. Why should a liberal state care about the cultural marketplace?

Let us suppose – plausibly, in my view[20] – that liberalism is a theory of autonomy in the sense that individual freedom is among the prime goals for a liberal society. Two further claims now immediately follow. The first is that a liberal society must be a *pluralist* society. There must be a sufficient number of truly different *options* to allow genuine personal choice, and these options must be such that agents can choose among them freely. Autonomy is empty without a range of 'choice-worthy' goals.[21]

The second claim is that, because it consists mainly of liberal individuals, a liberal society/state cannot be indifferent as regards the *content* of its own cultural setting. Liberal freedom is a historical achievement, not something that falls to us like manna from heaven, and it can only be maintained within certain cultural conditions.[22] To deny this is to presuppose that individuals and their agency can be conceived of as wholly detachable from any social setting; as being pre-socially constituted. This last position is commonly called "atomistic individualism".[23] It is a position that modern mainstream liberalism eschews, *pace* Michael Sandel et al.[24] But why should a liberal society consist of liberal individuals? Perhaps this is too strong a formulation, but it seems plausible to suggest that citizens in a liberal state must endorse some liberal values – e.g. individual freedom and formal or substantial equality – for the liberal project to succeed. At the very least, such citizens should not be openly hostile to the liberal project.

Taken together these claims imply that the options that must be available in a liberal society must be *of a certain kind* – they must be options that sustain and further liberal culture. What these options will be is not a question for philosophy alone. Sociology, psychology and the like will have a role here as well. Equally, common sense tells us that a society without universal basic education, a rich variety of arts and literature, and a certain amount of vivacity in the "marketplace of ideas", as Mill puts it, hardly qualifies as a liberal society at all; either that, or it will be a liberal society only for a very short period.

Historically liberals have been concerned about the workings of the (as they see it) behemoth of the state precisely because they regarded education, art and so on as institutions that are too important and too fragile for the state to handle. On the other hand, the mere acknowledgement of the importance and fragility of these institutions shows that a liberal state cannot consistently remain completely aloof vis-à-vis the cultural market. Its ongoing existence depends on a liberal society, and the claim that the liberal state should not care about the existence of the liberal state appears to display a certain internal tension. It has been pointed out to me that there is no inconsistency in saying: 'Given the conditions x, y and z of the social setting, let us be liberal, but given changes in conditions x, y and z of a kind undermining the social structure necessary for a liberal regime, let us be something else.' Granted, this is not inconsistent as such. Nevertheless, I hope that it strikes the reader as an extremely eccentric political notion. After all, the main reason why we engage in, or theorise about, politics must be in order to find certain states of affairs that are good (or right). One who champions women's rights will engage in politics, or in the theory of politics, in order to implement women's rights in a given society. The same must be true of defenders of other liberal values: these values are valuable, not just because they are valued by someone, but because they are good (or right).[25]

If we want to implement (or encourage or secure) rights or institutions that are valuable, we are also required to implement (or encourage or secure) the conditions those rights or institutions require to flourish. As Kenneth Westphal notes in a slightly different context: "Whoever rationally wills an end is rationally committed to willing the requisite means or conditions for achieving that end."[26]

So it seems that liberals must be concerned about the cultural setting after all. But concern for this is impossible if one is not prepared to take a definite stand on *the good*: without appealing to a conception of the good life – or at the very least, without raising controversial questions of a qualitative nature which cannot be answered purely in the abstract – we will simply be unable to determine what qualifies as art, what constitutes proper and sufficient education, and so on.[27] Thus, the neutral liberal state seems to be forced to take a stand on precisely those issues that it sought to avoid interfering with.

This conclusion, however, is too hasty. For it seems plausible that, in ideal circumstances, the liberal state need not interfere with the cultural setting after all. If the machinery of civil society continually provides society with meaningful, adequate and valuable cultural options and institutions, the state is not required to do anything in these areas. (Although it must still, of course, declare what exactly constitutes meaningful, adequate and valuable cultural options and institutions). Alas, such ideal circumstances are a contingent matter; as some liberals admit:

> Despite centuries of communitarian insistence on the historically fragile and contingent nature of our culture, and the need to consider the conditions under which a free culture can arise and sustain itself, liberals still tend to take the existence of a tolerant and diverse

culture for granted, as something which naturally arises and sustains itself, the ongoing existence of which is therefore simply assumed in a theory of justice.[28]

Suppose that high levels of literacy are a necessary condition of the ongoing existence of liberal society mentioned here. Suppose, furthermore, that we are dealing with a society where education is an entirely privately sponsored project; and where taxes providing for a basic level of education are not raised. Now, under ideal circumstances nothing forces the state to take any action whatsoever. But what is to be done if a whole generation of parents, or a large number of parents, decides that their children should not learn how to read and write?[29] Surely, this would undermine the future for any *liberal* culture.

It might be argued that Mill's harm principle justifies state action here, because the parent's more or less collective action dramatically narrows the range of options available to the illiterate, and thus harms them. Such an argument is essentially sound, but this fails to salvage neutrality: the state must take some coercive action (e.g. raising taxes, penalising non-compliant persons) and formulate a standardised canon (of what should be taught in schools etc.), but neither of these activities can be described without reference to what counts as good.[30]

Rawls seems to be aware of this: he notes[31], in passing, that the "…unavoidable consequences of reasonable requirements for children's education may have to be accepted, often with regret."[32]

> So even if we grant that neutrality and non-interference is a workable *ideal*, there are conditions – and these are normal conditions, moreover – under which the state cannot allow civil society to bear the burden of maintaining a liberal culture on its own. This is of course an empirical claim, but it is hardly a controversial one.

## VII. The Liberal Strategy: Civil Society as an Arbiter of Ideals

Turning, finally, to the liberal strategy, the question is this: is neutrality of justification compatible with state activity in areas in which the relevant judgements are non-neutral? Let us take it for granted that support for the arts is a kind of policy that a state would unqualifiedly wish to employ in order to maintain and further a specific culture. Let us also suppose that a liberal state could face a situation in which the cultural conditions needed for a genuine liberal society were threatened.

Kymlicka's response, which he stresses is in accordance with Ronald Dworkin's,[33] is this: in conditions under which state support is needed if we are "...to ensure the survival of an adequate range of options for those who have not yet formed their aims in life",[34] the state could pursue a policy of providing tax credits for those who support culture. Why does this not violate neutrality? Because, and this is the crucial point, "...the *evaluation* of these options occurs in *civil society*, outside the coercive apparatus of the state."[35] The argument could be repeated in connection with other areas of civil society: the same procedure could be applied to education, health care and so on.[36]

In essence Kymlicka, to some extent, and Dworkin, construct this strategy around the Rawlsian distinction between the public (the state) and the private (individual agents). The state cannot justify its actions by appealing to conceptions of the good, but individual agents, acting only on their own behalf, are expected to do this. Thus, civil society is 'the individual agent' writ large. Civil society is given an agency akin to the individual's. Therefore, justifications of policies in which reference is made to, and evaluations accord with, conceptions of the good, are permitted at this level.

It appears, then, that an active policy of protecting vulnerable and important areas in the cultural setting is compatible with neutrality after all.

The appearance is misleading. To see why, consider the following question: to *whom* are the means (raised by taxation in order to protect the aforementioned vulnerable areas in the cultural setting) to be distributed? If the state were to pick out specific persons and institutions directly, how could they avoid using perfectionist criteria of the good in deciding who should count as appropriate beneficiaries? Such criteria would obviously be involved in the case that the *state* picks out persons or institutions. Hence, Kymlicka and Dworkin – neither of whom would advocate something of this kind – must be proposing something like this: the state should either (i) distribute means (or give tax credits; this ultimately amounts to the same) to the whole of the cultural sphere; or (ii) employing a direct or electoral procedure, appoint boards of experts who allocate state funds to beneficiaries, be they persons or institutions.

In the first case, the neutralist state would face the problem of *defining* what counts as a person or an institution in the cultural sphere: clearly, literature is art, and therefore an element in the cultural sphere, but should all written material count as literature? Obviously, the Royal Shakespeare Company, or the Sydney Opera House, are institutions in the cultural sphere. Is mud wrestling as well? In a nutshell, the problem is that the state must take a stand on controversial questions about the *scope* of the cultural sphere; and this is incompatible with neutrality of justification.

In the second case, the neutralist state would face a dilemma. It could appoint boards of experts either directly or through popular mandate; or, as a variation on the second option, it could ask citizens to nominate institutions or persons that they felt were worthy of support.

In the first scenario, the original problem arises again. Surely, the state cannot be said to be neutral just because the day-to-day evaluation and 'micro-redistribution' of means is handled by experts appointed by the state itself. If the state wishes to avoid this unwelcome reappearance (or a higher-order use) of perfectionist criteria, it must find another solution.

In the second scenario, the state appears to be three steps removed from the actual distribution of means: it avoids any dependence on conceptions of the good insofar as it appoints neither beneficiaries nor experts directly; and it also avoids that dependence insofar as it stops short of determining the scope of the cultural setting.

However, the price paid for this is a recurrence of another original problem. For how can the state ensure that the allocated means are spent in supporting aspects of the cultural setting that it wished to support from the beginning? In my (admittedly, far fetched) example of the illiterate generation, *ex hypothesi*, citizens would not direct any received means towards support for literacy.

To summarise, the state is bound either to appeal to conceptions of the good in allocating means, or, to avoid this appeal, to remove itself entirely from the fray, and give up interfering in the contested areas. However, in the first alternative, neutrality of justification cannot be achieved; and in the second, the state gives up the power to ensure that the means it distributes are used in the intended way; to protect the societal framework and basis necessary for liberalism.

A rejoinder to this critique is available. The critique, it might be conceded, is by and large cogent, but the construal of liberal neutrality of justification given above misses the point. Neutrality is not about the state's *actions*. It is about its *basic structure*. The doctrine of neutrality applies only to the formation or construction of the basic institutions of the state. The rest – the actual workings of those institutions – is, as it were, up for democratic grabs. Thus, given a framework of reasonably just institutions, decisions about almost anything – including, of course, decisions about the support of the arts, education and so on – will be compatible with basic liberal intuitions.

This answer is not entirely without merit: it substantially reflects the actual practice of liberal democracies. A constitutional framework lays down certain constraints on the scope of democratic decisions, but leaves aside the day-to-day details to parliament, local or regional authorities, the political parties and so on. However, the concept of neutrality here is far removed from the concept of neutrality of justification as defined above. If democratic decisions made by the majority can lead to the implementation of particular ideals at a 'quasi-state level', then the state cannot possibly be described as possessing justificatory neutrality, no matter how neutral the constitutional framework. The rejoinder in fact trades on the confusion of a wide conception of neutrality vis-à-vis political and legal frameworks (this being a possible implication of neutrality as fairness) and the much more demanding concept of justificatory neutrality.[37]

A strategy in which civil society appoints a person or a board, perhaps by democratic decision, and this person or board distributes means provided by the state, is a non-starter.[38] Of course, it makes no difference if the democratic decision concerns practices, not a person or board. If such a policy were enacted, by the way, it would appear quixotic to insist on state-level neutrality. For if democratic decisions are allowed to dictate good-oriented perfectionist redistribution of the means of the state, why should democratic decisions about good-oriented perfectionist ideals not be allowed to enter the very heart of the state – the law and constitution– in the first place? Moreover, there is another problem with letting civil society handle the decisions. If the whole purpose of the state's actions is to provide support for threatened institutions in the cultural setting, what can the neutral state do if civil society decides to use the means the state provides it with to reduce the price of asparagus? At the very least, the state must have *some* idea of what is to count as the arts, what proper education is, and so on, and this again means giving up neutrality of justification.

It might be argued that the members of civil society, and thus civil society itself, should be neutral. After all, if the state should be neutral, why not the citizens? In other words, it would be morally wrong for the members of civil society to get involved in good-oriented perfectionist redistribution. Ackerman seems to advocate something along these lines, see Ackerman (1980). Such an all-encompassing neutralist thesis is, however, absurd. Neutrality must have limits of some kind, and to forbid the members of civil society to act, individually or collectively, in accordance with their conceptions of the good *as such* would be contrary to any plausible liberal intuition. It would also limit the individual's area of legitimate action to an unacceptable minimum: it would be inconsistent with personal autonomy.

Perhaps civil society can step into the role of saviour in another way. Bear in mind that liberal states will be required to maintain and/or further the cultural setting only under certain conditions, i.e. where valuable options are threatened and civil society cannot 'take care of business.' One of the main obstacles to such a predicament is probably the market. Free consumer choice tends to drive expensive choices out of the market in favour of cheaper ones. As a result of this, expensive cultural practices will inevitably be under pressure. Such practices might either wither away or become accessible only to well-off members of a cultural elite.

Now, modern liberalism as elaborated by Rawls, Dworkin et al., is undeniably *egalitarian*. These writers emphasise that the 'basic goods' of society (however conceived) should be distributed equally. It might be enquired, then: will not the egalitarian part of the liberal scheme function as a form of protection against the exclusion of the poor from important cultural practices? In other words, considering that one of the most important aims of modern liberalism is the fair distribution of assets to *all* members of society, is it likely that a situation will arise in which *valuable* cultural practices wither away? After all, such practices are only valuable if valued *by* someone, and if redistribution is fair almost everyone will have adequate means to sustain and further any practices that are truly worthy of furthering and sustaining.

I take the position that lies behind these questions to be what Dworkin calls the "economic approach" in his essay 'Can a Liberal State Support Art?'[39] This approach rests on the fundamental assumption that whatever goes on in an uncontrolled and thus, in the technical sense in which the term is used here, 'perfect' market is by definition a totally correct and fair reflection of consumer choice. I shall not go into the timeworn discussion that has attended this approach. It suffices to observe that Dworkin himself says that "…the connections between market prices and people's true preferences are not always so tight… [M]arket prices and transactions will not always be a fair measure of what the community as a whole really wants."[40] But if we grant, plausibly enough, that even where the distribution of means is relatively or completely fair, the market cannot act as a foolproof guardian of valuable cultural practices, then it follows that another solution must be found. In effect, Dworkin's essay argues for the view that the state should play an active part in maintaining and furthering valuable practices. However, he combines this with the suggestion that the policy should "...look to the diversity and innovative quality of the culture as a whole rather than to (what public officials take to be) excellence in particular occasions of that culture."[41] In other words, perfectionist ideals should be excluded from the justification of state policy.[42] Once again, civil society is invoked to play the role of arbiter. In view of this, we are back to square one, as shown above.

The conclusion remains the same, then: if the state wishes to take any action affecting the cultural setting, neutrality of justification must be given up. The strategy of letting civil society play the role of arbiter fails to salvage neutrality.[43]

## VIII. Conclusion

One conclusion has already been stated. This is that civil society cannot serve as a means through which the state takes action in the cultural setting whilst preserving its neutrality of justification. This does not prevent the state from excluding good-oriented perfectionist ideals. If everything goes well in the cultural marketplace, state action will not be called for. (Although the state will still of course need *some* criteria of what constitutes 'going well') This is one option: to hope, or simply claim, that whatever goes on in the cultural marketplace is just fine. If one chooses to go down that road, one embarks upon a journey likely to lead to libertarianism in one form or another.

The other option seems to be to give up on neutrality of justification and embrace perfectionist ideals in the justification of state policy. This is what so-called 'communitarian liberals' like Charles Taylor or 'perfectionist liberals' like Joseph Raz argue.

Perhaps these are the alternatives: neutrality of justification means that the state has two options. It can either seek assistance in handling matters of controversy – e.g. in deciding what curricula to have in schools, which institutions and persons should receive grants in the arts, what kinds of ailments and diseases we should pay special attention to in the health care system, and so on; or it can simply give up having a say in these matters. The latter option *is*, theoretically, an option. But the advocacy of such a minimal, libertarian state requires one to adopt a peculiarly barren political outlook. The former option – that of looking for *some forum* of decision – is a much more attractive idea. However, this forum cannot be truly neutral, so why not let that forum be the state itself? And that, of course, implies that (state) neutrality of justification has been given up.

It cannot be stressed too much, though, that this is in no way to suggest, or imply, that a liberal state should give up neutrality as an *ideal*. This caveat is especially important in view of the actual disagreement about what constitutes the good life among modern citizens of liberal states. In pursuing the ideal of neutrality the state need strive for neither consequential nor justificatory neutrality: the broader, but less demanding ideal of *neutrality as fairness* can be the target instead. Again, this means that at least some state policies must be founded on perfectionist ideals; but the precise demarcation of the areas of state policy that must be perfectionist under this or that circumstance is a problem yet to be adequately tackled. Furthermore, the problem of curbing (unjustified) state action so essential to liberalism – one of the main motivations for devising the concept of neutrality of justification – must be solved in some way without relying on that concept.

## Notes

1. I am indebted to the kind help and suggestions from colleagues at the institute for Philosophy, Education, and Rhetorics at Copenhagen University, especially Kasper Lippert-Rasmussen and Thomas Søbirk Petersen. I am also grateful for the scrupulous proof-reading of the original manuscript provided by Robinson at Lexicon Editorials and for the financial support the institute provided for this.
2. I use the term 'substantial' to cover any case of fairly concrete and precise action. Its opposite is 'formal'.
3. These are merely some very obvious examples. More complicated areas of state action could serve as examples, but blatantly 'ideological' areas of political action serve our purpose well.
4. For this, see Raz, pp.107ff; cf. Kymlicka (1989) pp.883ff.
5. *Mutatis Mutandi*, this consequential neutrality could be subdivided into the two categories of consequential neutrality that Caney calls *equal effects* neutrality (in which the state is neutral iff it has an equal effect on all conceptions of the good) and *equally easy* neutrality (in which the state is neutral iff it ensures that all conceptions of the good fare equally well). See Caney, p. 458
6. What I have in mind is the now widely accepted thesis that there is a tension between the "contractarian" and "intuitive" arguments in *A Theory of Justice*, and that we really should see the contractarian model as a heuristic device that illuminates the intuitive argument for equality. See Kukathas/Pettit, p.60ff, Kymlicka 1990, pp.55ff.
7. "The right is prior to the good", as this distinction is often sloganised. Readers familiar with the works of Rawls will know that his point of view turns from a universalistic to a more particularistic one in the later *Political Liberalism*. However, this change is a change in the scope of the candidates for his political strictures. Rawls acknowledges that certain cultural and economic circumstances must be present in societies fit for a Rawlsian theory of justice, i.e. his subject is, ceteris paribus, developed western society. The basic idea of neutrality remains the same. Readers who would argue that Rawls does not entertain the same notion of neutrality in his later works can read on keeping the older Rawls in mind only.

8. The doctrine of neutrality is endorsed not only by 'left-liberals' such as Rawls but 'right-liberals' or libertarians. Nozick provides a case in point: a state claiming allegiance by its citizens must be neutral in its dealing with those citizens. See, for instance, Nozick's *Anarchy, State and Utopia*, p. 33
9. To name just a few, Charles Taylor 1985, pp. 79ff and Michael Sandel, *passim*.
10. I use the term 'coercive' in an everyday fashion. I doubt that the term 'coercion' is put into proper use in most of out discourse about state action and law. State action and law are *not* necessarily coercive, and the claim that they are is not self-evident. See Edmundson, part 2.
11. One might hold that an action without consequences is not an action at all. For the difficulties of upholding a view of consequential neutrality, see Raz, pp. 110-33.
12. See Mulhall/Swift, pp. 29ff. Again, it does not matter whether the political process leading to the enactment of a policy is neutralist or not.
13. Kymlicka (1989), p. 884
14. For these arguments, see Kymlicka (1989), pp. 884ff. Note that no actual interference in, or judgement about, *particular* life-styles has been made by the state in the last example. If a life with much leisure and champagne turns out to be cheap, then so be it. See Rawls 1982. Thus Raz' quite bold proposition that liberalism rests on an idea of neutral political concern, especially in its tougher version (in which there is neutrality regarding the likelihood that a person will *adopt* one conception of the good rather than another), seems to be too quick.
15. And with him modern liberalism as such, see Kymlicka (1989) pp. 885ff, note 6. Kymlicka explicitly includes Nozick here.
16. Simon Caney, p.458, emphasis added. See also Mulhall and Swift, pp. 348ff.
17. Not because I want to link it especially with Rawls, although it is true that Rawls' justice as fairness could easily be re-interpreted to serve as an example of this notion. However, this would mean giving up neutrality of justification.
18. I take it that the postulation of such a link does not amount to the provision of an independent reason.
19. I shall use phrases such as 'cultural marketplace', 'culture', 'cultural setting' and the like to denote – *ceteris paribus* – the entire cultural, intellectual, educational, economical and religious framework of a society.
20. Utilitarian arguments for liberalism, in which it is claimed that liberalism maximises welfare, make an instrumental case for liberalism. I am not disagreeing with this instrumental view. It is simply beside the point in the present discussion.
21. Note that nothing here (yet) implies that it is the *state* that should guarantee or maintain these options. 'Pluralist' here does not mean 'relativist' or 'sceptical'. All it implies is the idea that autonomy is void without at least the possibility of different options. Even if the incredible situation should arise in which every member of society has the exact same goal, the *possibility* of realising alternative goals must remain genuine.
22. This line of criticism is pressed time and again by Charles Taylor. The basic premises for the attack are Hegelian: the liberal "sphere" of individual freedom is seen as the "sphere" of Kantian *Moralität*, but this cannot work without a proper cultural setting, an ethical and concrete *Sittlichkeit*. See Taylor 1975, pp. 376ff and Taylor 1979 pp. 113ff. It should be noted that the Hegelian strand of Taylor's thought works perfectly well without the more opaque metaphysical aspects of Hegel, as is convincingly argued in Taylor (1975).
23. See Taylor (1985b), p. 197; cf. Mulhall/Swift, p. 112. It should be noted that Taylor uses the term primarily in connection with the work of libertarians like Nozick.
24. What I have in mind here is that some of the communitarian critiques accuse Rawls et al. for holding an atomist thesis, but that such a critique misinterprets or confuses two different lev-

els of individualism, metaphysical and ethical. For this, see Kymlicka (1990), pp. 207-215, Kukathas and Pettit, pp. 11-16.
25. Raz puts this very bluntly: "For it is the goal of all political action to enable individuals to pursue valid conceptions of the good and to discourage empty ones", Raz, p. 133
26. Westphal, p. 247. Westphal is discussing the concepts of willing and freedom in Hegel and Kant at this point, but the claim in question reaches far into matters of the organisation of the state and the grounding of rights, and indeed more besides.
27. For a position that clearly says that the state should, under normal circumstances, support valuable and necessary institutions in the cultural marketplace, see Hurka, esp. pp. 158-60
28. Kymlicka (1989), p. 899; cf. Dworkin (1986), p. 225.
29. I am of course indebted to Rawls' discussion in (1993) pp. 195-200 and other places.
30. The raising of taxes in order to provide a *specific* kind of education *against* the will of agents cannot be fathomed merely by deploying the concept of the right, to the best of my understanding.
31. In Rawls (1993), pp. 199f, cf. Rawls (1988), *passim*
32. Rawls (1993), p. 200. See also Kukathas/Pettit, pp. 140f.
33. Kymlicka (1989), p. 895. Kymlicka refers to Dworkin (1986) chap. 11.
34. Kymlicka (1989), p. 894.
35. Kymlicka (1989), p. 895, emphasis added.
36. I should perhaps note that Kymlicka does not make this claim, although he does not say otherwise.
37. See the insightful discussion in Kukathas and Pettit, pp. 140-41, cf.: Rawls (1993) pp. 199-200. Rawls and his defenders often try to make a division between "constitutional essentials" and the "basic structure" on one hand, and "less important decisions", everyday political discussion and minutiae of the state administration on the other. In the first group, neutrality of justification should be upheld, whereas some (but not precisely defined) room for other considerations is left for the other. However, this "legal schizophrenia" does seem to be an *ad hoc* solution to the problems considered in this article. If the basic framework of law (the constitution) is neutral, and forbids non-neutral decisions to be made, then by hypothesis the full body of law must be neutral.
38. Consider this comment of Raz's about the doctrine of neutral political concern: "Government action should be neutral regarding ideals of the good life…This interpretation of the doctrine is silent on whether individual political action (voting in elections etc.) may rightly aim at the promotion of some conception of the good. Little attention has been paid to this as a separate issue in 'neutralist' writings" (Raz, p. 110 and note 2).
39. In Dworkin (1986), see pp. 221ff.
40. Dworkin (1986), p. 222.
41. Dworkin (1986), p. 233.
42. One might say that perfectionist ideals are already and necessarily in play when the state is obliged to evaluate what counts as 'the diversity and innovative quality of the culture as whole.'
43. Kymlicka himself notes that the use of non-state forums is not guaranteed to secure the necessary integration of citizens and cultural practices – that allowing civil society play the role of arbiter might not work out. "A culture which supports self-determination requires a mix of both exposure and connection to existing practices, and also distance and dissent from them. Liberal neutrality *may* provide that mix, but that is not obviously true, and it may be true *only in some times and places*" (Kymlicka (1990), p. 223, emphasis added).

## References

Ackerman, Bruce (1980) Social Jostice in the Liberal State (New Haven, Yale University press).
Caney, Simon (1991) Consequentialist Defences of Liberal Neutrality, *Philosophical Quarterly*, Vol. 41, issue 165
Dworkin, Ronald (1986) *A Matter of Principle* (Oxford, Clarendon Press)
(1989) Liberal Community, *California Law Review*, Vol. 77, No. 3
William E. Edmundson (1998) *Three Anarchical Fallacies* (Cambridge, Cambridge University Press)
Hurka, Thomas (1993) *Perfectionism* (Oxford, Oxford University Press)
Kukathas, Chandran and Pettit, Phillip (1990) *Rawls – A Theory of Justice and its Critics* (Cambridge, Polity Press)
Kymlicka, Will (1989) Liberal Individualism and Liberal Neutrality, *Ethics*, Vol. 99, No. 4
(1990) *Contemporary Political Philosophy* (Oxford, Clarendon Press)
Mulhall, Stephen and Swift, Adam (1996) *Liberals and Communitarians* (Oxford, Blackwell)
Nozick, Robert (1974) *Anarchy, State and Utopia* (New York, Basic Books)
Raz, Joseph (1986) *The Morality of Freedom* (Oxford, Clarendon Press)
Rawls, John (1971) *A Theory of Justice* (Oxford, Oxford University Press)
(1982) Social Unity and Primary Goods in: Sen/Williams (Eds.) *Utilitarianism and Beyond* (Cambridge, Cambridge University Press)
(1988) The Priority of Right and Ideas of the Good, *Philosophy and Public Affairs*, Vol. 17, issue 4
(1993) *Political Liberalism* (New York, Colombia University Press)
Sandel, Michael (1982) *Liberalism and the Limits of Justice* (Cambridge, Cambridge University Press)
Taylor, Charles (1975) *Hegel* (Cambridge, Cambridge University Press)
(1979) *Hegel and Modern Society* (Cambridge, Cambridge University Press)
(1985a) *Sources of the Self* (Cambridge, Cambridge University Press)
(1985b) *Philosophical Papers*, (vol. 2) (Cambridge, Cambridge University Press)
Westphal, Kenneth, (1998) Context and structure of Hegel's *Philosophy of Right*', in: Frederick C. Beiser (Ed.) *The Cambridge Companion to Hegel* (Cambridge, Cambridge University Press)

# THE VERY IDEA OF A BENCHMARK OF TRUTH

STIG ALSTRUP RASMUSSEN

I

In *Realism and Truth,* Michael Devitt confidently advances the claim that the Equivalence Thesis of Truth

(ET)   It is true that P, if and only if P

captures a minimum requirement of truth, i.e., any account of the concept of truth must accommodate this thesis. It is the very benchmark of truth[1]. This idea is widespread, and goes back at least to G. Frege, the early (and later) Wittgenstein and F.P. Ramsey[2]. If it is accepted, then it seems that there can be little quarrel with the Disquotational Schema holding for any declarative sentence, 'P', of any object language, L, as well:

(DS)   'P' is true-in-L, if and only if P.

Indeed, Crispin Wright takes (DS) to be derivable from (ET) and the stipulation that sentence 'P' express that P, in the exposition of his doctrine of minimal truth as the basic common ground for the combatants within a range of debates over realism and anti-realism[3].

So he, too, takes the view that (ET) captures the minimal core of any notion of truth. And although (DS), unlike the operator-formulation (ET), relativises the truth predicate to a specific language, he discerns no objection to letting (DS) stand in for (ET) in debates over the behaviour of truth. In view of some of the issues discussed below in Section III, treating (ET) and (DS) as more or less interchangeable is far from as innocuous as Wright thinks. However, the strategy in the sequel will be to ignore, as far as possible, the difficulties arising on this score.

Yet, there is every reason to be suspicious of (DS), as a general constraint on the truth predicate, if the notion of truth is to serve as a basis for an account of sentence meaning. That the notion should so serve is, of course, a Fregean idea[4]. Nowadays, it is common enough to accept the idea in the Davidsonian form, according to which to give an account of the meaning of the sentences of language L is centrally to put together a truth theory for L, the most notable feature of which is, precisely, that it churns out a theorem of the shape of (DS) – styled a T-sentence, in this role – for each sentence of $L^5$. Davidson's conversion of the Tarskian truth-definitional machinery into a theory of this nature has as its basis the idea that (DS) is mandatory for anybody occupied in accounting for linguistic meaning. That truth is subject to (DS) is supposedly obvious.

Tarski agreed that if anything concerning truth is obvious, then it is that (DS) must hold. Indeed, his sole constraint for ensuring the *material adequacy* of his semantical definition of truth for certain formalised languages was that the definition deliver instances of (DS), for each sentence of the formal target language $L^6$. The fact that these T-sentences within his definitional machinery result from assigning denotations to individual terms and satisfaction conditions to predicates is seemingly immaterial to the adequacy of the definition. His definition might, from that point of view, have taken the shape of a single definitional infinitary axiom schema, viz. (DS) considered in the manner suggested. The definition would however then evidently not have tied truth-in-L in any useful way to the semantical properties of sub-sentential structures of the sentences of L, and would therefore have forfeited its claim to much of the *point* it indoubtedly has[7].

Contrary to what seems to be suggested in Dummett's early writings[8], the Dummettian semantical anti-realist (or his creator) does not have to be presented as disagreeing with the above, although he will baulk at the suggestion that the core of linguistic meaning – the Fregean *Sinn* [9] – is exhaustively accounted for in this manner[10]. A usual claim, although it is not Dummett's, is that the anti-realist will have no quarrel with the truth – or assertibility – of (DS). He will, if T-sentences are to serve as meaning-specifiers for sentences of L, put restrictions on the interpretation of 'P', as this occurs on the right-hand side of the T-sentences. The P-specifications must be what Dummett calls 'full-blooded', i.e., they must proceed without overt appeal to those conceptual resources in the content of the thought that P in virtue of which that statement is thought worthy of being taken as anti-realistically problematic[11]. The anti-realist is however often supposed to have no further ground for reservations concerning (DS). But the validity of this claim will, as it turns out, depend on just how (DS) is construed.

## II

Now, on a semantical anti-realist account of meaning, truth will, for one reason or another, be gappy: on such an account, sentences not currently known to be effectively decidable (non-KED sentences[12]) will not enjoy determinate truth or falsity. That is, the Principle of Bivalence, thought of as an infinitary schema ('ß' being a metalinguistic variable for sentences of L)

(BIV)   ß is determinately true or ß is determinately false

will fail of general applicability within whatever sector of discourse is being subject to semantical investigation. The precise nature of the respective deviations from (BIV) depends on the specifics of such sectors. In general, however, the adoption of an anti-realist semantical account for a fragment of language will result in a logic weaker than standard classical logic, this being all that admits of semantical validation on anti-realist principles; and going beyond the logical means thus justifiable will be seen as inadmissible because not keeping faith with the meaning with which we can have endowed the expressions pertaining to the area in question[13].

Ever since Heyting offered the first axiomatisation of the logic underlying the mathematical practice of the intuitionists – codifying what Brouwer and he himself did, as it were – the question of what is the best account of that logic has been reasonably clear: it is intuitionistic logic[14]. Assuming that Dummett's account in semantical terms of that logic and of the language for which it is the logic are generally acceptable, the early intuitionists may be seen as forming one species of semantical anti-realist[15]. The characteristic semantical thesis of these is that (BIV) fails for non-KED mathematical sentences, e.g., Goldbach's Conjecture (and Fermat's Last Theorem, until Andrew Wiles turned it into a theorem). Such sentences are perfectly determinate as to meaning, just as are all other respectable mathematical sentences; but because mathematical truth is conceived of as (constructive) provability, sentences for which we have no present guarantee that we shall ever be able to decide their holding good or not cannot be accorded a truth value.

It should be noted that non-KED sentences are not, according to the above kind of anti-realist, supposed to fall into *determinate* truth-value gaps, as if the gap constituted a third determinate truth value on a par with truth and falsity. That kind of case is conceivable, too – indeed, it is the case treated of in Lukasiewics trivalent logic (the logic resulting from adopting trivalent semantics)[16]. The intuitionist rejects trivalence, just as he frowns upon bivalence. Indeed, he recoils from any principle of n-valence, for finite n, and he has no truck with more than the usual two truth values, truth and falsity. So, there can be, on his view, no *counter-examples* to (BIV). Indeed, it is intuitionistically incoherent to envisage that any wellformed mathematical sentence falls forever in a gap (apparent exceptions must, it seems, be explained as instancing deficiency of meaning[17]). This comes out nicely in syntactical form: although the law of excluded middle (LEM) does not hold for non-KEDs in intuitionistic logic, its double negation *is* a theorem of intuitionistic logic (just as are all double negations of sentential-logical classical theorems[18]). In short, the intuitionist anti-realist adopts *Agnosticism* in respect of the general applicability of (BIV)[19].

Another main type of semantical anti-realism arises over empirical statements, the notable feature of which is that they are, probably without exception, *defeasible*. For instance, ascriptions of mental states to others are anti-realistically true, roughly if and only if the criterial bases for their assertion are brought out by the observable behaviour of the (putative) persons in question, and nothing in the circumstances of their assertion recognisably indicates that the ascriptions should nevertheless be held in suspension. But the later identification of defeating circumstances is never precluded, and it is part of the understanding of the content of such assertions that defeating circumstances are envisaged as not to be ruled out[20]. Just how to contrive a formal semantics accommodating the latter feature is a moot point. It is however sufficiently clear that since truth is to be identified with assertibility in principle (of some sort), the resulting logic will presumably be no stronger than intuitionistic logic.

However, defeasibility is a real poser for the formal semanticist. It is obvious that assertibility, hence truth, cannot be *monotonous* in cases where defeators are abroad. That is, the assertibility now of 'P' does not ensure that 'P' will remain assertible in future. But although various proposals for dealing with non-monotonous truth values have been explored, notably in AI-research[21], nothing really satisfactory has so far turned up. One suggestion that might initially seem promising, that of Crispin Wright in his proposal to think of truth as *superassertibility*, does not seem quite to do the trick[22]. This is to the effect that a sentence 'P' is superassertible now, if and only if (i) it is assertible now, and (ii) it remains assertible in any future incremental extension of our present state of information, it being understood that our searches are to include both the pedigree of the assertion and how it fares with respect to more future-directed potential defeators. But now Wright must confront a dilemma:

Either we think of our assertion as holding up *in fact* under all future accretions of further evidence, or we think of its so doing being relevant to its superassertibility only if we can *now recognise* how its future history of (present) assertibility will develop. In the latter case it is difficult to see how superassertibility is different from present assertibility. On the former alternative, a superassertible statement is indeed monotonously assertible; but that is just to say that it is not defeasible. So, in either case the proposal fails to deliver the goods. The entire exercise looks like attempting to do Kripke-tree semantics for intuitionistic logic without the stipulation that if 'P' is forced at node n, then 'P' is forced at all nodes m, such that m>n. The whole structure essentially collapses into just one node[23].

The point still holds that the anti-realist, no matter how might be the genealogy of the truth-value gaps that concern him, is presumably constrained to be a revisionist in respect of logic[24]. Indeed, Wright has presented a neat argument to the effect that the anti-realist quite generally cannot have the law of excluded middle, if his anti-realism is supposed to reside in what Wright calls the Epistemic Constraint[25]:

(EC)    If 'P' is true, then it is feasible to know that P.

Now, it is in fact not entirely clear that the anti-realist can coherently assert (EC) quite generally. The so-called *Paradox of Knowability* takes us from (EC) and the assumption that there are hitherto not known truths straight to a contradiction. Timothy Williamson has powerfully argued that the anti-realist can have the major premiss, i.e., (EC). But this will be at the cost of dropping the assumption that there are unknown truths. This just may be bearable in the context, perhaps, since the assumption does not seem to have an expression in intuitionism[26] But, further, Williamson's resulting epistemic modal logic of the expression 'it is possible to know that' is outrageously non-standard[27]. I prefer my own view that the anti-realist's best way with the paradox is to abstain from asserting, *as well as denying*, the application of (EC) to non-KED sentences. There can, then, be no counter-examples to (EC). This agnosticism about the problematic instances of (EC) appears to me to be of a kind with the anti-realist's agnosticism with respect to the application of (BIV) to those same sentences[28]. The question now is whether Wright argument that anti-realism enjoins logical revisionism still goes through, if (EC) is replaced by agnosticism.

Well, it does not, as it stands. The principle of no counter-examples to (EC) is encapsulated in the claim that, for any P,

>   (NCEC)   It is not the case both that P and that P may not feasibly be known.

Classically, (EC) follows from (NCEC). Why not simply insert two substitition instances for 'P' (P itself and '-P', respectively) in Wright's proof and proceed as before? The trouble is that while the resulting derivation would satisfy the adherent of classical logic that the anti-realist must revise logic, it would have no force with the anti-realist himself, unless we picture this animal as being in a very special position, i.e., the position of inclining towards holding on to classical logic, but being open to allowing himself to be persuaded if presented with proof that he cannot. For the transition from (NCEC) to (EC) fails intuitionistically. However, the classical validity of Wright's proof, amended as suggested, may be sufficient to prove to everybody concerned, including the anti-realist, that the anti-realist cannot consistently hold on to the law of excluded middle. It would however be preferable if it were somehow possible to *stabilise* the position of the revisionist anti-realist by coming up with something similar to the improved Wrightean proof, but such that the proof held good intuitionistically. I do not at present see any way of doing this.

However, we know from the work of Dummett and others that the anti-realist presumably has no way of semantically making a case that he has a right to full classical logic. He can do no better that plump for intuitionistic logic. Furthermore, the improved Wrightean derivation proves internally that the would-be non-revisionist anti-realist is in trouble. It is no comfort to the non-revisionist that the improved Wright-argument fails to hold intuitionistically. For he is in no position to appeal to this fact. The only cost of simply concluding, on the strength of all this, that the anti-realist must adopt a logic no stronger than intuitionistic logic is the awkwardness that, once the anti-realist has done so, he is no longer in a position to accept his main reason for going revisionist. Still, he is pictured as prefering a position he will perhaps not after the fact be in a position to justify to a blatantly incoherent one. The principle behind this move appears to be unexceptionable.

We may conclude, then, that the anti-realist will be a logical revisionist. He will accept nothing stronger than intuitionistic logic. In the non-monotonic case we do not know that he may accept even that much logic. For present purposes, the consideration may however suffice that his position cannot accommodate anything beyond intuitionistic logic. Whatever additional damage to logic might be dealt by non-monotonicity will, if anything, serve to strengthen the points below, as they apply to this brand of anti-realist.

## III

What now of (DS)? It is clear that since (DS) contains a material bi-conditional the question must arise, once more than one logic is in play, how to construe this logical constant, along with further such constants as may occur in the various substitution instances of (DS). Of course, the constants are usually taken automatically to be classical. But on this reading, (DS) clearly is not available to somebody not entitled to this logic. To the anti-realist way of thinking, whenever 'P' is a non-KED sentence, the left-hand side of (DS) is false, while the right-hand side is of indeterminate truth value, on a classical reading of the bi-conditional. But this will not concern our anti-realist, who will of course insist on reading the bi-conditional intuitionistically. If he does, (DS) holds. For what it now says is that we have a way of recognising that any proof that 'P' is true constitutes, or can effectivele be transformed into, a proof of 'P', and *vice versa*. It is difficult to see how this could fail to be so. The upshot is that (DS) holds anti-realistically, as well as realistically. But why all the fuss, then? Because what seems to be often claimed is that *(DS) holds, or ought to hold, on a classical reading, even from the point of view of the anti-realist.*

Of course, nobody ever put forward the claim in the form just stated. Nevertheless, the anti-realist is in a roundabout fashion put in a position of being to blame for being unable to accept (DS), or some descendant of that principle, the reading of the principle being tacitly classical. The usual procedure is to propose an anti-realist 'improvement' of (DS), along the lines of

(ARDS) 'P' is assertible, if and only if P.

It is then suggested that there is a genuine question as to whether the anti-realist can really have (ARDS), as he is thought to require if truth is some kind of assertibility. It is further suggested that the anti-realist cannot have (ARDS), and that the situation is to be improved upon by trying out some fancy improvement on straight 'assertibility'. For instance, assertibility is required to be 'warranted', or to amount to 'superassertibility', or the like. These putative strengthenings seem however to be of no avail. But there is no mystery. The anti-realist can perhaps have (ARDS), just as he can definitely have (DS), if the bi-conditionals are thought of as he must indeed think of them – as intuitionistic. Otherwise he plainly cannot have either of the two principles. By the same token, (ARDS) is no improvement on (DS), from the anti-realist point of view. On the contrary: the proposer of (ARDS) is likely to be in a serious muddle over what should be said metalinguistically in the semantics of L and what should be represented – as an operator or a predicate – in L itself. The anti-realist has every title to (DS), and he wants no other principle.

It is quite another matter that the *realist* will want a way of characterising the position of the revisionist anti-realist. In this regard, the situation is illustrated beautifully by Gödel's mapping of intuitionistical sentential logic into *classical* modal logic S4[29]. The modal necessity box is to be read as 'intuitonistic provability'. And as Gödel points out, we do precisely not get 'If it is intuitionistically provable that P, then P' as a translation of anything expressible in intuitionistic logic. It fact, if this were a theorem in the theory resulting from the translation, then 'P' would be provable for all P, i.e., intuitionistic logic would be inconsistent. Further research into this precise point led Martin Löb to his famous theorem[30]. This all seems very odd, perhaps, but the main source of the apparant oddity has in fact nothing as such to do with intuitionistic provability. The difficulty of reflecting provability in the object language – the language in which the sentences are stated and of whose provability is treated – will invariably lead to the result that 'If it is provable that P, then P' will not be assertible (i.e., not a theorem, in the case where provability is meant to be provability in some theory stated in the object language). Gödel in fact discovered Löb's theorem for the special case of intuitionistic provability, considered as an object-linguistic operator. At least, I see no other way of interpreting the concluding few sentences in his very short paper.

In the general anti-realist case before us, things are much the same. To think that 'true' in (DS) ought somehow to be replaced with 'assertible', or the like, in order that (DS) be anti-realistically palatable, is a blunder, unless it goes with an attempt to construe 'if and only if' as a *classical* bi-conditional. If it does not, such 'improvements' on (DS) may perhaps be admitted as a way of putting an anti-realist gloss on his thinking about the principle, but the reformulations are more likely to simply mislead and ought to be avoided.

However, it is a legitimate concern to attempt to make sense, in realist terms, of anti-realist thinking about (DS) and related principles. This is not merely to serve the debate between the combatants on either side of realism/anti-realism debates, who naturally will make little headway unless their respective positions are comprehensive to both parties involved. The theoretical aim of the semanticist who wonders how logical laws might be justified – or criticised – pulls in the same direction: the metalinguistic characterisation of the competing positions must not be allowed to beg the question against the adherent of either classical or intuitionistical logic. So, there is an inherent theoretical interest in semantical characterisation that will not simply result in the logic of the object language being automatically decided by the logic of the metalanguage – as a mere reflection of the logic underlying the semanticist's reasonings. Furthermore, there is some indication that the ambition of make realist sense of the anti-realist is not inherently hopeless: as Dummett points out, it makes little difference whether we reason classically or intuitionistically when employing Kripke trees as a way of (perhaps somewhat inadequately) providing a formal semantics for intuitionistic logic[31].

Suppose, then, that the anti-realist position is to be characterised in a language the underlying logic of which is classical. How will (DS) and (ARDS) now stand, the bi-conditional being read as classical, but any semantical machinery being taken to be acceptable to the anti-realist? Well, (DS) as we know will fail. (ARDS), or any considered improvement of that principle, is bound to fail for the very same reason Gödel could not allow 'If it is necessarily the case that P, then P' as a theorem resulting on his mapping from intuitionistic logic into classical S4: if a principle of that nature were in force, then the overall position would be inconsistent. We should refrain from jumping to the conclusion that anti-realism admits of no semantical characterisation in which classical logic is operative. We may however conclude that (DS), along with its more or less happy descendants, will not form part of that characterisation.

The position as to the Paradox of Knowability – touched upon in the above – is much the same. The major premiss (which is identical to (EC)) is that, by the anti-realist's lights, if P, then it is possible to know that P. But is the conditional classical or intuitionistical? Well, the natural view to take is that it is classical and that the conditional is supposed to say something, which the anti-realist would put *intuitionistically*. The conditional does not, however, seem to map anything of that kind. But, on the alternative reading of the conditional, that premiss appears to be an uneasy hybrid between, on the one hand, something an anti-realist might wish to say in intuitionistic terms and, on the other, an attempt to spell out classically what he is saying. The anti-realist does *not* wish to put modal or epistemic operators into his – intuitionistic – conditionals of the sort under discussion, because his conditionals are *already* intensional. Gödel's mapping hammers this home, if we had not noticed before[32].

So, it is not clear that the major premiss makes any anti-realist sense at all. But if it does, it must be that of ruling out that a sentence may be true and yet not knowably so. This was the line I took above. Taking it involves treating the logic in play as, at the strongest, intuitionistic logic, since otherwise the distinction collapses between my preferred reading and the one just pronounced a hybrid. In short, the anti-realist has it that there can be no counter-examples to the major premiss, as read intuitionistically; but the realist will have no way of preventing an acceptance of this intuitionistic stance from coinciding with a declaration of the falsity of the contested major premiss. So, that premiss in no way captures the gist of anti-realism.

It is simply a blunder to overlook the above, and the repercussions can be felt high and low. For instance, Wright fails to take any notice of these matters in his discussion of how the Negation Equivalence

(NE) 'P' is not true-in-L, if and only if 'not-P' is true-in-L.

is both classically and intuitionistically derivable from (DS) – part of his case for attributing more content to the latter than is allowed by various deflationists about truth[33]. His clarifying (second) derivation goes like this[34]. By (DS) we have that 'P' is true, if and only if P. By contraposition, 'P' is not true, if and only if not-P. By (DS) again, not-P, if and only if 'not-P' is true. So, 'P' is not true, if and only if 'not-P' is true. This all holds intuitionistically as well as classically.

Wright is correct in claiming for his derivation that it goes through even intuitionistically. And it is perfectly true that the anti-realist actually wishes to endorse (NE), although Wright evidently finds it hard to believe this fact[35]. But there is again no mystery. When the anti-realist endorses (NE), (DS) and Wright's derivation, he simply reads *all* of it intuitionistically. What makes Wright initially baulk at his result is that, like many others, he neglects to construe (NE) and (DS) intuitionistically. Classically, the anti-realist cannot have either of them. Just to see why he cannot accept (NE) on this reading of it, consider the case of a non-KED sentence, P, which enjoys no anti-realist truth value. The right hand side of (NE) is then true; but the left-hand side is not, since the negation of an indeterminate sentence itself has no determinate truth value.

There is a line of objection to the above that cannot be ignored. It is this. In the treatment, above, of truth value gaps, it was alleged that the anti-realist is an agnostic with respect to the principle of Bivalence, considered as a schema – that *absolute* truth value gaps have no place within his view of things, and that these, in so far as they nevertheless appear to occur (e.g., the Continuum Hypothesis might seem to fall into such a gap), the phenomenon is to be anti-realistically discounted as owing to deficiency of meaning, on the part of the gappy sentence. How about Gödel sentences, though – sentences saying of themselves that they are not provable within given, consistent extensions of Robinson Arithmetic? Such sentences will provably be neither provable nor refutable within the respective systems their own provability properties in which these sentences pronounce upon[36]. So, do not these sentences fall into permanent gaps, from the point of view of the anti-realist?

Related to this question is that, if the appeal to Gödel and Löb in the above is supposed to create trouble of the kind outlined for Wright and others who believe, e.g., that the anti-realist position is best captured by (EC) and 'improvements' on (DS), why cannot a similar worry be raised for the *realist*, when he is depicted as taking it, as part of his position, that (DS) holds, on a classical reading of the material bi-conditional. After all, Tarski's indefinability theorem precludes there being a truth predicate for theory T (again T is any consistent extension of Robinson Arithmetic)[37]. Why should this theorem not be thought to rule out that even the realist adherent of classical logic can have (DS)? And if it does not, why cannot the anti-realist have (ARDS)?

These worries are connected. Note, first, that a truth predicate, in the sense of Tarski's theorem, does not capture the realist's notion of truth, since the latter is not in the least supposed to be tied to any particular theory, or theories. Truth-in-T, for some theory T, falls short of truth-in-L, even if T is expressed in language L, unless the L involved is extremely restricted. Furthermore, the realist's notion of truth is supposed to be absolute, in the sense of being independent of what is or is not provable in any, or every, theory. When he propounds (DS), he takes truth in this informal and comprehensive sense. So, he is not vulnerable to objections against (DS) derived from Tarski's indefinability theorem, unless his notion of absolute truth can quite independently be made out to be somehow incoherent.

The position is partly analogous, partly quite different, when we turn to consider the the anti-realist adherent of intuitionist logic. He shares with the realist classicist the view that there must be a notion of absolute truth – truth as transcending any given theory of anything. Indeed, Gödel's first incompleteness theoren proves that arithmetic is indefinitely extendable, in that it will, for any given consistent arithmetical theory T, always be possible to produce by Gödelisation a true sentence not provable in $T^{38}$. But any given Gödel sentence can always be absorbed as provable in a successor theory to T: just add the sentence to T as an axiom. This is why it makes sense to rule out anti-realistically acceptable *absolute* gaps arising over Gödel sentences, although the sentences possess fully determinate meanings.

However, the anti-realist's position is very different from that of the realist, when it comes to trying to make sense of absolute truth values. It is tempting to say that if we cannot appeal to Tarski's indefinability theorem to prove the realist wrong in endorsing (DS), then surely we ought not appeal to the Gödel mapping and Löb's theorem in order to debunk anti-realist 'improvements' of (DS). The theorems are, after all, proved in much the same way, by diagonalisation. But this is wrong, on two counts.

First, although the Gödel mapping results in Gödel nearly stumbling on Löb's Theorem, the establishment of the result that the mapping works does not involve the diagonalisation machinery. Second, even if anti-realist truth is not to be identified, or explained in terms of, provability in any particular formal theory, the notion cannot be separated from all links with provability in some theory, however informal and remote. Determinate truth values and gaps are not on a par, as they would be to a realist adherent to trivalence. The position is not symmetrical in regard of truth values and gaps. Sentences are *established* (by proof or production of reasons for thinking that proofs will be forthcoming) to enjoy determinate, permanent truth values; but they are never in this sense established to fall into gaps. The main point is that, as a consequence, the Gödel mapping and the Löb theorem will be in force no matter what level of theorising we consider. To think otherwise of anti-realist truth values – that at some ultimate level things will be different – is, at best, to construe all anti-realist talk of truth as an attempt to say the ineffable. So, (ARDS) remains a piece of hybrid nonsense.

## IV

The noteworthy fact is that there is something to the claim that (DS) holds, on several views. As it happens, that principle holds on the preferred view of just about anybody, as long as the bi-conditional is construed in terms of whatever logic is valid for the object language L. Since that is the logic one is unthinkingly taking to hold, principles like (DS) really do look rather platitudinous and yet not entirely devoid of content; and this is no doubt one reason why (DS) has seemed to so many to be the very benchmark of truth. But the principle means different things to different people; and that is why it is not in itself – as a perfunctorily understood piece of syntactical scribble – terribly informative. Wright, in his attempt to get significant mileage out of it – in part to prove the various deflationist conceptions incoherent, in part to assist in his constructive efforts to set up a basis on which to conduct realist/anti-realist disputes – trades on (DS) being no doubt anti-realistically true on one reading, and a lot more interesting on another – on which, unfortunately, it fails.

Furthermore, Devitt's onslaught on Dummett's entire enterprise misfires grievously, because he thinks the anti-realist can have no title to (DS) or a descendant couched in terms of assertibility[39]. But beating the anti-realist about the ears with such principles is to little avail. The anti-realist can have either, but is best advised to stick with (DS) itself. The following remarks by Dummett are worth bearing in mind when engaging in thought about truth[40]:

> .......we have no guarantee that the notion of truth which we need for these purposes [those of the theory of meaning; SAR] will be one for which each instance of the (T) schema is correct..........the schema (T) will fail for any notion of truth which does not commute with the logical constants, in particular negation, and hence for any under which we have reason to say that a sentence may fail to be true without its negation being true.

The lesson of the above is that we should not expect to find a 'benchmark' of truth in abstraction from the role which we contemplate for that notion, both generally and, more specifically, in the theory of meaning. Wittgenstein was probably right that the concepts of *truth* and of *proposition* are acquired as a pair, and remain notionally interdependent[41]. It is from this interdependence we might be able to destill a core of what truth must, at the very least, of necessity be. It is, of course, far from clear that (the later) Wittgenstein would have taken his observation to imply anything more substantial than 'platitudes' such as (DS); but we, who in the light of Dummett's work are better equipped, are free to think otherwise. And, after all, the narrow intuitionistic notion of a proposition (let alone a more general anti-realist one) stands in need of elucidation

## APPENDIX

Wright's elegant proof that anti-realism leads to logical revisionism is (slightly reorganised) this:

| | | | |
|---|---|---|---|
| (1) | P v -P | | (LEM) |
| (2) | P -> It is possible to know that P | | (EC) |
| (3) | -P -> It is possible to know that -P | | (EC) |
| (4) | P | | A |
| (5) | It is possible to know that P | | 2,4, MPP |
| (6) | It is possible to know that P v It is possible to know that -P | | 5 vI |
| (7) | -P | | A |
| (8) | It is possible to know that -P | | 3,7 MPP |
| (9) | It is possible to know that P v It is possible to know that -P | | 8 vI |
| (10) | It is possible to know that P v It is possible to know that -P | | 1,4,6,7,9 vE |

So, (LEM) combines with (EC) to lead by intuitionistic, hence also classical, logic to a result best seen as a demonstration that all sentences are decidable. But they are not, in fact; and if they where, semantical anti-realism would be pointless – at least in its Dummettian form. So, non-revisionist anti-realism is incoherent.

The adjustment contemplated in the text is to insert two instances of (NCEC) into this proof and derive from these the two instances of (EC) occurring in lines (2) and (3). Classically, this works; but intuitionistically, it does not. So, a would-be non-revisionist anti-realist is in a position to comprehend the incoherence of his position; but he will, for all the argument shows, be unable to endorse the reasoning establishing the incoherence of his previous position, once he has abandoned classical logic.

Incidentally, Wright fails to notice the interesting fact that the validity of his argument is unaneffacted by whether the would-be non-revisionist anti-realist is a Dummettian molecularist or a semantical holist. Suppose the anti-realist endorses classical logic, including (LEM), on the strenght of holist considerations. Even if his anti-realism is supposed to reside in adherence to (NCEC), rather than in (EC), his would-be non-revisionism obliterates any benefit the anti-realist might have hoped to derive from this; and Wrights argument proves that his position is incoherent, unless holism puts him into the position of being able to endorse the non-existence of non-KED sentences. In short, the holist can have classical logic, only if holism somehow ensures the existence of a guarantee that absolutely any sentence is decidable. This argument strenghtens the case for rejecting anti-realist versions of holism, since if there were such a guarantee, why adopt anti-realism?

## Notes

1. M. Devitt (1984), Ch. 3. Something like Devitt's view of this seems to be shared almost universally; cf., e.g., P. Horwich (1990), Ch. 1.
2. G. Frege (1918), p 345; L. Wittgenstein (1922), 4.024 ; F.P. Ramsey (1927), pp. 44-45; and L. Wittgenstein (1997), § 136.
3. C. Wright (1992), Ch. 1-2, cf. especially pp. 33-37. Devitt does not seem to distinguish (DS) from (ET); cf. M. Devitt, *Op. cit.*, p. 24.
4. G. Frege (1918), pp. 344-45.
5. D. Davidson (1967).
6. A. Tarski (1983). Nothing in the remarks below in any way affects the correctness or seviceability to its purpose of Tarski's work. He succeeds completely in achieving exactly what he sets out to do.
7. The possibility of so framing the definition, but now considered in its role as a paradigm for a Davidsonian theory of meaning, is broached in C. Wright (2001b), pp. 44-45.
8. M.A.E. Dummett (1978), Essay 1.
9. G. Frege (1892).
10. M.A.E. Dummett (1978), 'Preface' marks the shift from seeing the anti-realist as *rejecting* the notion of truth as the central notion in semantics to one who *reinterprets* truth as assertibility.
11. M.A.E. Dummett (1975), pp. 101-02.
12. This terminology was introduced in S.A. Rasmussen & J. Ravnkilde (1982), p. 389. I believe J. Ravnkilde came up with the expression.
13. For the general idea of this, cf. Dummett (1978), Essays 14 , 17 and 21, and M.A.E. Dummett (1991), Ch. 8-9.
14. A. Heyting (1930); cf. also A. Heyting (1971), Ch. VII.
15. M.A.E. Dummett (1978), Essay 14 and M.A.E. Dummett (2000), pp. 1-21 and Ch. 7.
16. J. Lukasiewics (1967).
17. The Continuum Hypothesis might be thought to be a counter-example – to (BIV) as well as to the claim in the text. But the combined results of Gödel and P.J. Cohen seem to me to leave nothing further to investigate, as set theory as now formulated is concerned. We can have the Continuum Hypothesis or not, just as we please and in accordance with present concerns. If we share with Gödel a nagging feeling that there simply must be a fact of the matter, this could be interpreted as a call for further *precisification* of our notion of a set. So, the gap is owing to indeterminacy of meaning, not fact. Cf. Gödel (1940) and P.J. Cohen (1966).
18. Cf. D. Scott *et al.* (1981),p. 189-69.
19. I believe the first precise occurrence of this point in the literature is in S.A. Rasmussen & J. Ravnkilde (1982). C. Wright replied to this paper; cf. C. Wright (1993), Essay 16. This reply, in turn, provoked S.A. Rasmussen (1990).
20. C. Wright (1993), Essays 12 and 13.

21. Cf. the comprehensive reader M.L. Ginsberg (1987).
22. C. Wright (1993), pp. 414-15; and C. Wright (1992), pp. 48-61.
23. S.A. Kripke (1965). Cf. M.A.E. Dummett, (2000), pp. 134-37, and N. Tennant (1978), pp. 106-13 and 132-34.
24. Unless, that is, he thinks that semantical holism holds to the extent that *all* logical laws – truths and inference rules – are constitutive of the meaning of the logical constants. I follow Dummett's rejection of this doctrine, at least to the extent of ignoring it in the sequel; cf. M.A.E. Dummett (2000), pp. 252-55.
25. C. Wright (1992), pp. 41-42; C. Wright (2001a), pp. 65-69, especially note 24. Wright's two proofs are not identical. The more recent proof is to the effect that (EC) leads, intuitionistically as well as classically, to the result that the law of excluded middle holds only for decidable sentences. Cf. Appendix.
26. M. Dummett (1991), p. 78.
27. T. Williamson (1992).
28. S.A. Rasmussen (1997).
29. K. Gödel (1933).
30. M. Löb (1955); Cf. G.S. Boolos & R.C. Geoffrey (1989), pp. 187-88, and G.S. Boolos (1979), Ch.1.
31. M. Dummett (1991), p. 26.
32. One reason for failing to notice the (weak) intensionality of the intuitionist 'material' conditional is that it is of course subject to the so-called paradoxes of material implication. The fact deserves note that it is so, only because special provisions are made to ensure that it is. Once the eliminability of double negation is dropped from classical logic, the law (or rule) of *ex falso quodlibet* is not derivable. This is then specifically added as a primitive rule to ensure, precisely, the derivability of the 'paradoxes' in intuitionistic logic.
33. C. Wright (1992), pp. 19-21 and 31-32.
34. *Ibid.*, Ch. 1. It seems that the deflationist has a short answer to Wright's imputation to him of a commitment to a view concerning the interrelations between 'truth' and 'assertibility': the deflationist could simply deny that he holds, or ought to hold, any such view. As far as truth is concerned, (DS) is (nearly) the whole story, he will claim; and when assertibility is the issue, that invites totally unrelated considerations of an epistemological nature. This may not in the end be a plausible view (it is not!); but Wright does not seem to advance considerations that force the deflationist to abandon his trench.
35. *Ibid.*, pp. 41-43. Wright makes great play with (NE) being *forced* upon the anti-realist by his acceptance of (DS). Part of the trouble is that Wright tends to state (NE) using an operator-formulation. If this is written out as a classical S4 formula, taking 'true' to mean 'intuitionistically provable', it fails to translate anything in intuitionistic logic, and the formula is in any case invalid in S4. So, that formulation does not even hold in the paradigm case. In the predicate-formulation given here, however, (NE) reflects the behaviour of negation in Kripke trees.
36. K. Gödel (1931). Cf. G.S. Boolos & R.C. Jeffrey (1989), Ch. 14-16.
37. This theorem is the main result in A. Tarski (1983), as presented in modern texts. Cf. G.S. Boolos & R.C. Jeffrey (1989), pp. 176 and 188-89.
38. Cf. M.A.E. Dummett (1978), Essay 12, for a discussion of the resulting position in mathematics.
39. For M. Devitt's onslaught, cf. his (1984), Ch. 12. Devitt airs numerous misgiving about Dummett's work, in addition to the one discussed at this point in the text. I find most of them simply preposterous. Still, Devitt's book is an admirably clear statement of a kind of realism that probably enjoys widespread support.

40. M.A.E. Dummett (1991), p. 64. Notice that the point about (T), i.e. our (DS), is put in terms of what holds or not on the assumption that we reason classically in the metalanguage.
41. L. Wittgenstein (1997), §§136-37.

Literature

Berka, K. & Kreiser, L. (eds.) (1983) *Logik-Texte* (Darmstadt, Wissenschaftliche Buchgesellschaft).
Boolos, G.S. (1979) *The Unprovability of Consistency* (Cambridge, Cambridge University Press).
Boolos, G.S. & Jeffrey, R.C. (1989) *Computability and Logic*, 3rd ed. (Cambridge, Cambridge University Press).
Cohen, J.L. (1966) *Set Theory and the Continuum Hypothesis* (Reading, Mass., W.A. Benjamin).
Davidson, D. (1967) Truth and Meaning, *Synthese,* 17, pp. 304-23; repr. in: D. Davidson (1984), pp. 17-36.
Davidson, D. (1984) *Inquiries into Truth and Interpretation* (Oxford, Clarendon Press).
Dummett, M.A.E. (1975) What is a Theory of Meaning, in: S. Guttenplan, *Mind and Language* (Oxford, Clarendon Press).
Dummett, M.A.E. (1978) *Truth and Other Enigmas* (London, Duckworth).
Dummett, M.A.E. (1991) *The Logical Basis of Metaphysics* (London, Duckworth).
Dummett, M.A.E. (2000) *Elements of Intuitionism*, 2nd ed. (Oxford, Clarendon Press).
Frege, G. (1892) Über Sinn und Bedeutung, repr. in: G. Frege (1967), pp. 143-62.
Frege, G. (1918) Der Gedanke, repr. in: Frege (1967), pp. 342-62.
Frege, G. (1967) *Kleine Schriften* (Darmstadt, Wissenschaftliche Buchgesellschaft).
Ginsberg, M.L. (ed.) (1987) *Nonmonotonic Reasoning* (Los Altos, California, Morgan Kaufmann).
Gödel, K. (1931) Über formal unentscheidbare Sätze der *Principia mathematica* und verwandter Systeme I, *Monatshefte für Mathematik und Physik*, 38, pp. 173-98; repr. and Engl. tranl. in: K. Gödel (1986), p. 144-95.
Gödel, K. (1933) Eine Interpretation des intuitionistischen Aussagenkalküls, repr. with Engl. transl. in: K. Gödel (1986), pp. 300-02.
Gödel, K. (1940) *The Consistency of the Continuum Hypothesis* (Princeton, New Jersey, Princeton University Press).
Gödel, K. (1986) *Collected Works*, Vol. I (New York, Oxford University Press/Oxford, Clarendon Press).
Heyting, A. (1930) Die formalen Regeln der intuitionistischen Logik, *Sitzungsberichte der Preussischen Akademie der Wissenschaften,* Physikalisch-mathematische Klasse, pp. 42-56, abbr. repr. in: K. Berka & L. Kreiser (eds.) (1983), pp.188-92.
Heyting, A. (1971) *Intuitionism*, 3rd ed. (Amsterdam/New York/Oxford, North-Holland).
Horwich, P. (1990) *Truth,* (Oxford, Blackwell).
Kripke, S.A. (1965) Semantical Analysis of Intuitionistic Logic I, in: J.N. Crossley & M.A.E. Dummett (eds.), *Formal Systems and Recursive Functions* (Amsterdam, North-Holland), pp. 92-130.
Löb, M.H. (1955) Solution of a Problem of Leon Henkin, *Journal of Symbolic Logic,* 20, pp. 115-18.
Lukasiewics, J. (1967) On Determinism, in: St. McCall (ed.), *Polish Logic 1920-39* (Oxford, Clarendon Press), pp. 19-39.
Ramsey, F.P. (1927) Facts and Propositions, in: F.P. Ramsey, *Foundations* (London and Henley, Routledge & Kegan Paul) 1978.

Rasmussen, S.A. & Ravnkilde, J. (1982) Realism and Logic, *Synthese,* 52, pp. 379-437.

Rasmussen, S.A. (1990) Supervaluational Anti-realism and Logic, *Synthese,* 84, pp. 97-138.

Rasmussen, S.A. (1997) Vidensparadokset ('The Paradox of Knowability', in Danish), Filosofiske Studier, 17, (Copenhagen, Institut for Filosofi, Pædagogik og Retorik, Københavns Universitet), pp. 140-60.

Scott, D. *et al.* (1981) *Notes on the Formalization of Logic* II, (Oxford, Sub-Faculty of Philosophy, University of Oxford).

Tarski, A. (1983) The Concept of Truth in Formalized Languages, in: *Logic, Semantics, Metamathematics,* 2nd ed. (Indianapolis, Indiana, Hackett), Essay VIII, pp. 152-278.

Tennant, N (1978) *Natural Logic* (Edinburgh, Edinburgh University Press).

Williamson, T. (1992) On Intuitionistic Modal Epistemic Logic, *Journal of Philosophical Logic,* 21, pp. 63-89.

Wittgenstein, L. (1922) *Tractatus Logico-Philosophicus* (London, Routledge & Kegan Paul) (1971 repr. used).

Wittgenstein, L. (1997) *Philosophical Investigations,* German/English 2nd ed. (Oxford, Blackwell).

Wright, C. (1992) *Truth and Objectivity* (Cambridge, Mass./London., Harvard University Press).

Wright, C. (1993) *Realism, Meaning and Truth* (Oxford, Blackwell).

Wright, C. (2001a) On Being in a Quandary, *Mind,* 110, pp. 45-98.

Wright, C. (2001b) *Rails to Infinity* (Cambridge, Mass./London, Harvard University Press).

# ON BRANDOMIAN APORIA (AND ONE WAY OUT)

TOMÁŠ MARVAN

Department of Education, Philosophy and Rhetoric
University of Copenhagen
marvan@flu.cas.cz

In his book *Making It Explicit*, Robert Brandom has presented us with a fresh vision of how a pragmatist inferentialist might try to tackle many substantial philosophical problems: so many that the expectations of even the most daring of the inferentialist creed are surpassed. But we all also know that a great philosopher possesses the qualities of being imaginative and thought-provoking, not necessarily the quality of being right. In this paper I draw attention to one of the central thoughts of Brandom's book, the one the author himself acknowledges to be in danger of circularity. This concerns how to explain the content of a concept. I will argue that the threat of circularity is indeed real, going on to suggest one possible way of resolving the matter without jettisoning Brandom's pragmatist and inferentialist insights.

## I

One of Brandom's truly original contributions concerns his systematic treatment of two central inferentialist notions: that of a *materially-correct inference* and that of the *content* of a concept. To see these notions as closely connected is not absolutely novel, of course. Brandom here draws primarily on the work of Wilfrid Sellars and on his pioneering idea of a "logical space of reasons", whereby some of the very central philosophical notions like that of knowledge are treated in a thoroughly normative fashion – their *inferential* substance is sought.[1] If we ask what it is for someone to know something, we should not look, according to Sellars, for an answer that would specify a kind of *state* that the person is in, but should instead look for inferential *grounds* that lead the person to the given conclusion.

Brandom starts with the Sellarsian picture and develops it into its full pragmatist-inferentialist form. Concerning the two notions mentioned, he seeks to *explain* the notion of the content of a concept by means of the notion of a materially-correct inference. First, then, we must be clear about what exactly a materially-correct inference is. This notion is distinct from the notion of a *formally*-correct inference in that it deals with the non-logical content of the concepts used in the given inference. Thus, to infer from the fact that a house is painted red to the fact that it is coloured is to engage in a piece of materially-correct inference, even though from the formal point of view there might be nothing to say about this inference. We could just as well say that whereas formally-correct inferences preserve the truth of the propositions involved in them, materially-correct inferences are, in addition, *content*-preserving. Now, it is obvious that Brandom needs a way of explaining the notion of a materially-correct inference without relying on the notion of the content of a concept. Otherwise he would be trapped in a circle: he would be presupposing precisely what he wants to explain. To this end, he introduces a third crucial element into his picture. This is the deeply-pragmatist notion of a *practical attitude towards an inference*, being carried out by a member of some discursive community; this attitude splits into the acceptance of an inference and its refusal. Brandom then suggests that we define materially-correct inferences as such inferences that are *treated as correct* in the actual discursive practice of its users.[2] The inference that 'if a house is painted red then it is coloured' is materially correct *because* it is taken as correct in the actual practice of the speakers of English. This explanatory move clearly indicates why Brandom takes himself to be a member of a distinguished tradition of pragmatist thought: the crucial features of human rationality manifested in our use of linguistic expressions and concepts are, on his account, traced back to what we actually *do*.

So far, so good. It is only when we start to wonder *why* it is that people actually do endorse some material inferences and reject others that we begin to feel rather uneasy in the framework of explanation just sketched. The crucial question becomes this: What kind of *abilities* must be granted to discursive creatures like ourselves? As far as I can see, one could reply to the question in two different ways. One could declare that (1) materially-correct inferences are taken as correct due to their content. This would mean crediting speakers and their interpreters with a grasp of the content of concepts that is prior to their actual discursive moves. This, however, is a position Brandom is clearly not entitled to take, on pain of circularity; his approach is rather to secure the emergence of the content of a concept as a result of the discursive moves. Alternatively, one could try a much bolder claim that (2) by endorsing some material inferences and rejecting others, people are not applying an already formed content of concepts but literally *establish* or *create* those contents by their actual attitudes towards inferences. (Let me call this position 'content creationism' henceforward).

This idea might sound a bit odd, but Brandom apparently should endorse something like it if he prefers to avoid explanatory circularity. Of course, he could also try to modify his official explanatory strategy, but let's suppose he won't give that up early on. In the history of philosophy, position (2) bears a close structural resemblance to Descartes' conception of absolute divine will, according to which the good is what God wills, not vice versa; God is therefore not determined to treat some things as good (or bad) in advance of particular acts of his own will.³ In the same vein, according to content creationism people are not determined to treat inferences as correct (or incorrect) in advance of their actual acts of endorsing them. In this picture, they would have to issue their endorsements or denials of inferences *blindly*, so to speak.

Talk about the "blind" application of rules sounds familiar in contemporary philosophy, of course. Wittgenstein uses this expression in his discussion of following (or "obeying") a rule.⁴ He thinks that we cannot follow explicit rules *according to* other explicit rules: we would then need other rules telling us how to follow these second-order rules and so on *ad infinitum*: the regress of rules would never terminate. His way of putting it is nevertheless not entirely satisfactory and is subject to the same scruples we have in Brandom's case. If we take the expression "blindly" literally, we will attribute to him a view of rule-following that I call content creationism. To follow a rule blindly in this sense would mean to apply it *from scratch*, without any prior knowledge of how the rule is to be followed. This kind of 'darkness' is, of course, all too dark. On this reading our application of rules is quite arbitrary in the sense of being unpredictable. And if it is unpredictable, it makes no sense to talk about the *correctness* of its application. But Wittgenstein apparently *wants* to speak about correct application of rules. One way to summarize his well known discussion of private rule-following is to say that the crucial evidence against the possibility that someone follows a rule privately consists in the fact that such an individual would not have the resources to distinguish between correct rule-following and what only seems to him to be correct rule-following. Wittgenstein must correspondingly mean something different by the term "blindly." Of course, the alternative reading is obvious. Wittgenstein meant by "blindly" something like 'automatically'. We follow rules in a habitual way, because we were trained to do so. We do not demand a further explication of their content. Hence, we do not follow rules from scratch: we have a *practical* know-how.

As I have remarked, Brandom should endorse something in the spirit of content creationism which emphasizes blind application of concepts in the literal sense of the term. But notice that its acceptance would clash with another part of his inferentialist strategy, viz. with the Kantian thought that concepts are rules that *bind* us to apply expressions in judgements in a certain way. "We don't possess concepts, concepts possess us", is one of Brandom's favourite slogans, repeated a number of times in his works. One way to resolve the tension here would be to modify the original Kantian position, claiming that *first* we establish the contents of our concepts in our actual practice in the manner of concept creationism, and only *then* do we bind ourselves to apply the contents thus established in our judgements. But such a treatment would not do anything to remove the stigma of the original arbitrariness of our judgments and concept-use. And Brandom has a sophisticated inferentialist account of the concept of *objectivity* in our judgments and so should reject the idea of content creationism.

What, then, is the option Brandom wishes to take? He seems to have in mind a solution that would avoid the problems of option (1),[5] of option (2) that we labeled "content creationism" and of yet another position to be specified. Let me start, then, with the options he explicitly rejects. In fact, Brandom has his own title for (1): he calls it "regulism" and attributes it to Kant.[6] According to regulism, we apply concepts in judgements on the basis of our knowledge of their fully established and explicit content; the knowledge is considered to be prior to the actual acts of using the concepts in judgements. Brandom avoids this position for the very Wittgensteinian reasons mentioned above: he thinks that adoption of regulism leads to a danger of infinite regress. (On the other hand, he wants to adopt parts of Kant's normative approach to concept-use, as indicated in the last paragraph; this has some consequences we will appreciate below.) Another Brandomian term, "regularism," marks a further position he tries to avoid.[7] This is a, roughly, Wittgensteinian position but not quite the one I have called content creationism. Regularism tries to account for the application of rules and concepts by reverting to the whole community of discourse participants and its regular discourse behaviour. Here we have our option (3) then: according to regularists a correct application of rules or concepts gets checked by what kind of judgements the community regularly issues.[8] The content of concepts or rules might also be taken as arbitrary on this picture, but not as arbitrary as in that of content creationism. It is arbitrariness relativized to the whole of the discursive community (and hence it is at least *interpersonal*) and moreover a kind of repeatable (and hence also predictable) arbitrariness. But, as already stated, Brandom prefers objectivity to arbitrariness and so does not want to stop at the level of what (almost) everybody in the community does. His notion of objectivity is in this sense speaker- and interpreter-attitude-transcendent. Moreover, he complains that regularism blurs the distinction between "treating a performance as subject of normative assessment of some sort and treating it as subject to physical laws". (Brandom 1994, p. 27)

So Brandom tries to avoid regulism, content creationism and regularism. Let's speak now about what Brandom embraces. His prefered way of characterizing the approach that is to escape the dangers of the positions mentioned involves the notion of 'the implicit'. He claims that by endorsing inferences people *implicitly* apply certain concepts. But, despite my desire to speak about the positive content of Brandom's doctrine, it is almost exclusively in negative terms that I am able to say what it means to have an implicit grasp of a concept. To apply a concept implicitly is not to have an explicit statement of the content of a given concept in mind while applying it. It is not a theoretical ability. What *can* be said about this ability in positive terms is this: to have an implicit grasp of a concept is to be able to participate in a kind of *praxis*. The Brandomian notion of an implicit application of concepts thus resembles the Wittgensteinian notion of blind rule-following in the second sense of automatical or habitual application. The explicit characterization of concepts comes, according to Brandom, only later, after their implicit content is already firmly established in some discursive practice.

Now, to return to the problem stated earlier in this section: does Brandom's account thus manage to remove the danger of explanatory circularity? Well, since an implicit grasp of the content of an inference might still be legitimately taken as a grasp of its implicit *content* – and Brandom should be able to do without any prior grasp of the content of concepts – the answer seems to be negative. The position based on the notion of the implicit is hence also not entirely satisfactory, given Brandom's stated explanatory objectives. And there is another, independent source of worry that strengthens the suspicion that Brandom's account of conceptual content via the notion of practical normative attitudes of discursive creatures doesn't work. This is the distinction between the *actual* and *ideal* attitudes of speakers and their interpreters towards discursive inferences. Brandom, as we have seen, speaks about the content of concepts being established by what people actually do in the discursive situations. But the question is rather what kind of inferences they *ought* to accept or reject – otherwise we would end up with something close to option (3), regularism, a position Brandom rejects. If the characterization of Brandom's position given in this paper is correct, the position is reductivist. It reduces the ideal normativity of concept use to the actual normativity of normative discursive attitudes of speakers and interpreters. But this, again, is not consistent with Brandom's idea of the attitude-transcendent objectivity of conceptual content.

## II

So far I have indicated some of the problems in Brandom's account of conceptual content and pointed to roads he is not willing to take. In the remaining part of this paper, I want to do two things. First, I will outline one of the important sources of the explanatory strategy that Brandom sketches (attempting to explain the notion of a materially-correct inference by means of endorsements of it by speakers and interpreters) and I will indicate in which way it may give rise to false explanatory expectations. Second, I will suggest what I think is a sensible way of using Brandom's inferentialist insights – without, however, commiting myself to the *aporia* spelled out in the preceding section.

To my mind, one of the most important sources of Brandom's official explanatory strategy is his overall description of the pragmatist inferentialist project in *Making It Explicit*. Brandom wants to conduct the inquiry first from the perspective of an *external* interpreter, who studies 'from without' the linguistic behaviour of members of a given discursive community. After due time and pains, the perspective of an external interpreter merges with an internal perspective of native speakers and interpreters.[9] The interpreter achieves this by registering the patterns behind their particular "inferential moves" and by thus reconstructing the contents of their concepts. But notice here the same sort of difficulty that we stumbled upon earlier. Brandomian external interpreter can only tell us *that* such and such moves are being taken, not *why* they are being taken. If we ask now why the participants endorse certain material inferences and refuse to endorse others, we find ourselves at once in the midst of troubles already mentioned. From the external interpreter's point of view the tracking of inferential moves (by means of a sort of a *deontic score* that at every particular stage of the discourse assigns to each participant a list of what she or he is inferentially committed to and entitled to by her or his particular inferential moves[10]) might well be the only way of determining the contents of concepts used. But we would also, and primarily, like to know what are the abilities and knowledge that *enable* speakers and interpreters to participate in some discursive practice in the first place.

I am suggesting, then, that it is Brandom's focus on the perspective of an external interpreter that is primarily responsible for various tensions in his inferentialist position. But let me now briefly avert some possible misunderstandings. I do not want to suggest that it must *always* be a problem to see how an external interpreter can eventually succeed in capturing the meaning of natives' utterances and other acts. In fact, people like Quine and Davidson have quite elaborate stories about how such a process works. They start on the level of basic observation sentences, correlating the natives' utterances directly with observable features in their surroundings. Once this "entering wedge of language" (Quine's expression) is captured, the systematical reconstruction of other parts of natives' language follows. It might be noted here that Davidson, who accepts the basic Quinean framework, could quite easily join forces with Brandom. He has a comprehensive account of the causal nature of linguistic interpretation, but, in addition, he holds that assignments of meaning and other propositional attitudes are governed by the principles of rationality that are broadly inferentialist in nature. Brandom and Davidson say in many places virtually the same thing: in other places they complement one other. I have particularly in mind Davidson's inferentialist statement of how the referentiality of propositional attitudes is co-determined by their inferential relations. Correspondingly, in Brandom we find the same idea in his denial of "representationalist" theories of propositional content, i.e., theories that hold that the representational element of propositional attitudes precedes and determines the inferential one.[11]

When I said that the perspective of an external interpreter is primarily responsible for the problems mentioned, I had in mind only *Brandom's* peculiar version of it. It is a mystery how a Brandomian external interpreter could ever penetrate into the natives' discourse. Brandom usually speaks as if it is a matter of course that the external interpreter knows what the natives are talking about. But would the interpreter be really *external* – we need to be told how he even *begins* to be able to work on his deontic score for interpreting the natives; unless I am mistaken, he simply cannot start to register particular inferential moves from scratch. Put in a nutshell, Brandomian theory is in strong need of some non-inferential (presumably causal) procedure that would enable the inferential one in the process of interpreting the behaviour of the natives.

Now, given the methodological problems with Brandom's position we dealt with, what might a reasonable solution look like? In the first place, Brandom would do better to drop his idea of *explaining* the notion of a materially-correct inference by means of the notion of the practical attitudes of speakers and interpreters toward inferences. This would, of course, in part reduce the explanatory ambitions of his inferentialist project, but, as indicated, his official way of explaining the content of concepts doesn't work; quite the contrary, it seems to create more problems than it solves. The real merit of Brandom's attempt lies in showing the close relationship between the notion of the content of concepts and that of a materially-correct inference, *not* in explaining the first one by means of the second. The problem, of course, is to give this relationship an appropriate name. What one can correctly say is that speakers and interpreters *manifest* their knowledge of the content of concepts by endorsing or refusing particular material inferences. Brandomian interpreter can work up his deontic score because the deontic moves of participants of some discursive practice lie in the open. As a kind of action, they are palpable. But, unless we are ready to accept the implications of content creationism (and few of us are, I suspect) we will conclude that the notion of a practical attitude towards an inference is too weak to bear the explanatory weight assigned to it in *Making It Explicit*.

This proposal also has some implications for the methodology of an external-interpreter-point-of-view. As far as I can see, Brandom is in danger of confusing *understanding* and *explanation* in his book. An external interpreter (enamoured of the Quine-Davidsonian way of penetrating natives' speech) might well achieve an understanding of the natives, but it is hard to see what would give him the license to *explain* what motivates their behaviour at the same time – to explain, that is, their grasp of the content of concepts they use. I would therefore suggest a partial revision of Brandom's description of his inferentialist project. Tentatively and rather melodramatically, I would suggest that we take Brandom's deontic score-keeping interpreter not as a wandering stranger ("field linguist" or what have you), but as a sage who *already is* a member of some discursive community and who is able effortlessly to participate in its linguistic practices. We might then keep the rest of Brandom's description of our sage's mission: his job is *to make the implicit discursive moves of his discursive tribe explicit*. This would mean crediting him with the task of giving a comprehensive account (in the manner Brandom is so good at) of which normative categories bind our linguistic behaviour and how. In case Brandom does not consider this reduction of his explanatory ambitions acceptable, he must show that the notion of a practical attitude towards an inference can, after all, bear the explanatory weight he assigns to it in his account.

Freed of the obstacles created mainly by the adoption of the perspective of an external interpreter, Brandom's approach has many riches to offer. To return to the rhetoric of the initial paragraph of this paper, the move suggested here would not only enable him to remain imaginative and thought-provoking, but also vastly enhance his chances of being *right*.[12]

## Notes
1. See Sellars 1997, esp. § 36.
2. See Brandom 1994, pp. 132-134.
3. See, e.g., Descartes' *Reply to the Sixth Objections*, § 6. (Adam and Tannery 1996, vol. VII, pp. 431-433).
4. See Wittgenstein 1958, § 219.
5. According to which we apply concepts in judgements endowed with a prior (explicit) grasp of their content.
6. See Brandom 1994, pp. 18ff.
7. *Ibid.*, pp. 26ff.
8. I do not intend to step here into the difficult question of whether Wittgenstein is a regularist or not.
9. For the description and the metaphor of a merger see Brandom's interview with Susanne Schellenberg (Schellenberg 1999).
10. See Brandom 1994, part I, sec. 3.IV.
11. Compare Davidson 1984, p. 168, and Brandom 1994, p. 93f.
12. I thank Jaroslav Peregrin and Stig Alstrup Rasmussen for stimulating discussions and criticisms and to James Hill for improving my English.

## Bibliography
Adam, C. and Tannery, P., eds. (1996) *åuvres de Descartes* (Paris, Vrin).
Brandom, R. (1994) *Making It Explicit* (Cambridge, MA, Harvard University Press).
Davidson, D. (1984) *Inquiries into Truth and Interpretation* (Oxford, Clarendon Press).
Schellenberg, S. (1999) Von der Begriffsanalyse zu einer systematischen Metaphysik, in: *Deutsche Zeitschrift für Philosophie*, 47, 6, pp. 1005-1020.
Sellars, W. (1997) *Empiricism and the Philosophy of Mind* (Cambridge, MA/London, Harvard University Press).
Wittgenstein, L. (1958) *Philosophical Investigations* (Oxford, Blackwell).

# IS REASON COMMUNICATIVE?
# SOME CRITICAL REMARKS ON HABERMAS

PETER WOLSING

Department of Philosophy
University of Southern Denmark
e-mail: wolsing@filos.sdu.dk

Below, I intend to sketch out a criticism of a basic claim in the philosophy of Habermas, namely that reason is essentially communicative. I intend to argue that Habermas' replacement of the so-called consciousness-oriented paradigm with a communicatively based one is untenable. Or more precisely: – that *reason* is not a social construction, even though it makes a unification of human individuals to a community possible by virtue of its universality. Furthermore, it is the purpose of my argument to keep Habermas' strong concept of reason as a real, a socially unifying power but at the same time to show that his grounding it "in der Praxis der Lebenswelt" – in language, action, cooperation and history[1] – is no convincing alternative to the philosophy of consciousness and the metaphysics of Antiquity. Reason par excellence is not the same as consensus; on the contrary: by virtue of its universality reason is what makes consensus possible.

## I. The young Hegel as an Example

Habermas extracts his concept of rationality from a variety of complicated contexts which comprise philosophy of language, of action and sociological and historical analyses. Here I just focus on moral reason as the basis of a stable community, or in the words of Habermas: of the 'ethical totality'. In this context the ideas of the young Hegel play a significant role. Even though Habermas construed his theory of communication on a basis which professes to mark a break with Hegel's philosophy of consciousness, i.e. on the premisses of 'the linguistic turn', he is still generally inspired by the idea of a totality in its mild communicative version in the young Hegel: "In Hegels Jugendschriften war [...] die Option, die sittliche Totalität als eine in intersubjektiven Lebenszusammenhängen verkörperte kommunikative Vernunft zu explizieren, noch offengeblieben. Auf dieser Linie hätte eine demokratische Selbstorganisation der Gesellschaft [...] treten können"[2]. Consequently, there is a potential to a theory of communication in the thought of the young Hegel. Though in Habermas the means are being provided within a theory of communication the objective is the same as in the young Hegel: at stake is a concept of reason which makes the difference of safeguarding unity, coherence and humanity in modern societies.

Following the critical view of the age in 'Frankfurter-Hegel', Habermas claims that from the outset modern society is characterised by a social list. This tendency Hegel called *'Entzweiung'*, referring to the social atomising and alienation which accompanied market economy, political liberalisation and materialism. But most of all he alludes to the loss of meaning which resulted from religion losing its power in line with the general secularisation of society and culture. Following Hegel's view of his age Habermas too considers it the most important task of modern society to support a 'unifying' countermove to the tendency of *'Entzweiung'* in modern societies. The expression morality does not only cover virtues to be practised individually and privately in order to counteract social injustice; a theory of morality must always keep the social and cultural totality in view and provide the conceptual means which makes it possible to take measures against actual dissociations and atomising powers in order to equalise differences.

But whereas the young Hegel still believed in the unifying potential of religion against the dissociations created by the market powers and by political individualism, Habermas holds the view that re-establishing the totality, the community, presupposes reason and morally qualified enlightenment. The pivotal point of such an ethical orientation towards totality can be detected – according to Habermas – in the communication which is always already active in all forms of human life practice.

## II. Reason as Communication?

The young Hegel was a modern theorist insofar as he rejected the metaphysical idea of order in the antique tradition and instead attempted to think ethical life (*'Sittlichkeit'*) on the basis of intersubjective relationships. But he did not go far enough. According to Habermas, a modern theory of social community must be detached from religion and be founded on communicative reason as it unfolds in the diversity of practical contexts of daily life. But though Habermas is not blind to the contributions of religious culture to humanity, it is his general view that communicative practice as it actually unfolds in modern liberal societies of itself possesses the resources to create and protect democratic and humane societies. Here he focuses on the unifying aspect of communication.

In the theory of communication of Habermas, the ethical sphere is an integrated part of the rational behaviour which characterises all forms of knowledge, dialogue and practical cooperation. A concise formulation sounds like this: "Verständigung wohnt als Telos der menschlichen Sprache inne "[3]. Here Habermas not only means the understanding of an expression but a *mutual* understanding with the person who utters it, i.e. he means consensus. So communication amounts to more than just an exchange of attitudes. It becomes a moral task. On the other hand, this connection of morality to communication means that morality becomes a basis insofar as it, so to speak, lives by the rationality inherent in communication. Habermas says that communication – insofar as it not only aims at understanding a statement but at an agreement – can be traced back to an old 'logos' idea which rests on the "...zentrale Erfahrung der zwanglos einigenden, konsensstiftenden Kraft argumentativer Rede, in der verschiedene Teilnehmer ihre zunächst nur subjektiven Auffassungen überwinden und sich dank der Gemeinsamkeit vernünftig motivierter Überzeugungen gleichzeitig der Einheit der objektiven Welt und der Intersubjektivität ihres Lebenszusammenhangs vergewissern"[4].

Now the question is whether this discursive foundation of morality can comply with the claim of a consensus based on reason which it promises. In other words: provided that we opt for a universalist view on morality – which Habermas does[5] -, is reason – which alone has the power to create consensus – to be considered as dialogue, or as discourse when understanding breaks down? This question touches upon the status of reason. More precisely, from the perspective of the history of philosophy, it has to do with how Habermas understands *reason* in relation to the 'strong' metaphysics of Antiquity and to the grounding of it in a modern philosophy of consciousness.

It is a step in Habermas' attempt to understand the modern condition as a post-metaphysical age that he wants to weaken the antique idea of identity by transforming it into a rational dialogue between free and equal partners. But he struggles on another front too, namely against the philosophy of consciousness from Descartes to Fichte[6]. In this tradition – and very much so in Fichte – knowledge and morality are based on autonomous subjectivity as intellectual performances, i.e. as an allegedly original act which is brought about by subjectivity and transcends the determining influences of the outer world. What Fichte realised was that morals do not simply reproduce a superior divine order but that the human individual begins with the consciousness of himself in relation to the natural world and freely produces his moral relations. Together with other free persons he thereby creates another world, *'Sittlichkeit'*, a realm of freedom above the natural world of unconscious, determined processes.

According to Habermas, it is a problem that this theory results in a categorical opposition between man and world. As the individual constitutes itself as a subject, he leaves his healthy position as 'one among others' and places himself opposite, outside the world. The theory overlooks a third sphere between subjectivity and objectivity, namely the social practice which – according to Habermas – can be described without falling into the problematic dualistic model: In social practice, we work our way out of the restraints of the outer world, of nature, and at the same time we discover freedom in the affirmative relationships to each other which communication cunningly creates.

In relation to the metaphysical concepts of reason in Antiquity and in the philosophy of consciousness, Habermas intends to bring back the individual to the world and to community, calming him with the argument that reason is already at work there: in our rational doings, in our daily dealings and in linguistic interaction with each other. It is just a question of finding the proper starting point for thought (philosophy of language, theory of action) and of working out the proper conceptual tools – then we make reason visible as a feature of the life world.

In relation to the metaphysics of Antiquity, it is not so much Habermas' intention to eliminate as to *explain* metaphysics, proving the origin of its idea of unity in social and rational processes. In relation to the philosophy of consciousness he claims something like this: the theory of communication and of the common life world provides the theoretical background for raising the individual back to a social self-understanding after he has loaded himself with the burden of making himself the world-constituting subjectivity. Habermas kindly removes his self-imposed burden of being the origin of reason and demonstrates to him that his epistemic and moral performances after all live on knowledge and competences which have already been produced by history and which serve as the resources for a further development of society and culture.

But is Habermas capable of presenting a positive alternative to the tradition of metaphysics and to the philosophy of consciousness? Does his communicatively based ethics not draw on the strong concept of reason which is represented by the tradition that he wants to take his leave of? The question sounds like this: What is the status of reason? A unity in the manifold as in antique metaphysics; a performance of subjectivity in the shape of individuality, or is it the consensus reached at through a discourse according to certain rules?

Below I intend to suggest the – actually well-known – view that reason is not the same as rational discourse; on the contrary, it is a reason beyond human individuals which is a condition that makes consensus succeed. This reason is at work in the dialogue and it appears in the subject as thought. Reason is metaphysical insofar as it is the instance which makes each participant in a group able to correct himself – and last but not least: the group too can correct itself on its basis. Also Habermas recognises this! As regards having a well thought-out point of view, being able to argue for it and applying language to communicate it to another competent user of a language – all this is a rational *activity*. In this activity I stake my own subjective opinion in order to end at a view which can claim universal validity. Therefore communication with another person can succeed. Here the rational kernel is the universal which makes it possible for two 'separated' interlocutors to build a bridge between them.

Now, it is interesting to notice that Habermas' view of the demands of validity in morality almost coincide with this description of reason as transcending the individual. Participation in a discourse also implies the cultivation of virtues like being open to all parties involved in the actual matter and submission to the coercion of the better argument etc. The reason in the discourse thus amounts to entering the space of publicity, to letting one's opinion be tried through arguments, in short: reason consists in being self-correctingly minded vis-à-vis the matter in hand through a cognitive activity which unfolds itself as a discourse. What role does consensus play here, then? For Habermas it plays a significant role: Through the discourse we arrive at an agreement or at a true community which *is* morality itself. But the reason for Habermas' unconditional confidence in the discourse seems to stem from the fact that he ties the discourse to a reason which must *exist in itself* insofar as it can act as a correcting, trying instance for the subjective opinions of various individuals. Reason transcends individual and group in the sense that it makes mutual understanding possible; it builds a bridge between separated individuals. Habermas' confidence in the discourse is based on a strong concept of communicative rationality, namely on the "experience of the unifying, consensus-founding power of arguing speech". Are there not traces of the concept of identity in these words?

The metaphysical idea of unity also seems to be at work in the ultimate purpose of communication: The agreement in view almost appears in the shape of harmonic identity, as a unification of separated constituents (to use an expression from Hegel). The mutual understanding which the rational dialogue holds up for itself as an ideal is characterised as the symmetry in the mutual recognition of communicating partners, in the harmonic interaction of their speaking and listening, and these virtues of the dialogue cause the differences of the individual subjects to fade away, so that the "unity of reason can be sensed in the diversity of its voices". How far is there from the idea of 'reciprocity', 'equality', 'symmetry' to the idea of a harmonic identity which in Antiquity indicated the reality of the metaphysical unity? The expressions Habermas applies are more than just metaphors; they point to the "consensus-founding *power* of rational speech" [my italics, pw].

So far, Habermas' distance from the metaphysical tradition does not seem that great. It should be evident that in both camps there is an idea of reason beyond particular differences at work: In Habermas as the reason inherent in communication; in Antiquity as the unity experienced through pure thought.

### III. Fichte´s subject – solitary and self-asserting?

But not even the probably most radical philosopher of the Cartesian tradition, Fichte, should be excluded from the noble gathering. The philosopher of subjectivity does not deprive reason of being universal and communicative just because it is connected to the so-called 'original act' (*'Tathandlung'*) of the subject. Indeed, it is a fundamental problem in Fichte's 'Doctrine of Science' that as soon as the 'I' constitutes itself, it also constitutes its Other in the shape of an objective 'offence' (*'Anstoss'*) which cannot be integrated in the subjective sphere. Consequently, he did not succeed in building a bridge between subject and the world. But Fichte's problem is probably only methodological. Thereby I mean that the system developed in the 'Doctrine of Science' at least has an intention which the point of departure of the system does not really make transparent. (Hence his endless attempts to start all over again). However, this true intention of Fichte's work was to 'call for' an insight in which the individual and the universal are a unity. Fichte considers it the privilege of idealism to unify these two: "Er [der Idealismus] fordert den Zuhörer oder den Leser auf, mit Freiheit einen bestimmten Begriff zu denken; werde er dies, so werde er finden, dass er genötigt sei, auf eine gewisse Weise zu verfahren. Es ist hier zweierlei zu unterscheiden: der geforderte Denkakt: dieser wird durch Freiheit vollzogen [...] – und die notwendige Weise, wie er zu vollziehen ist; dies ist in der Natur der Intelligenz gegründet, und hängt nicht ab von der Willkür; sie ist etwas *Notwendiges*, das aber nur in und bei einer freien Handlung vorkommt {...}"[7].

So what Fichte really refers to through his constant call to the individual to liberate himself from the attitudes of other's (the attitude of dogmatism) and to think, is probably the trivial experience that the specifically human, namely reason, only exists as an act: that it must be *produced* by every single individual again and again in order to *be*. But when it *is* – for instance when its subject has made himself a participant in a discourse – this produced reason is indeed universal in the trivial sense that the individual person subjects the content of his speech to certain criteria of validity, i.e. tacitly presupposes that his claims can be substantiated and thus be valid as true or normatively right. Without being able to live up to these demands the claims, of course, are not universally valid.

Hence the noun 'subject' does not refer to a particular individual who divides the community by maintaining his arbitrary attitudes and interests. On the contrary, as essentially being the subject of an act of reason it can only be the will of the individual who knows himself, to unite with the community through the universal, liberating himself from his particular life. As subject he simply becomes "ein Tun [...] nicht einmal ein Tätiges [...] Es kommt [...] ihr auch kein eigentliches *Sein, kein Bestehen* zu"[8]. In his *'Tathandlung'* the individual person does not leave the community; on the contrary, he *de*substantiates himself as a particular in favour of the in-and-for-itself rational which upholds the community. Hence it is a misunderstanding on the part of Habermas to assert that 'subject' means the particular individual; on the contrary, it more likely refers to the aspect of *production* in reason, i.e. to the fact that only through the act of the individual can reason become reality.

Fichte's concept of reason makes it possible for reflection to distinguish the *content* from its being produced and thereby to focus on the universal in and for itself. According to his words above, the content of reason amounts to the necessity by which reason proceeds; this could be the valid argument which constrains consensus. Fichte's discovery thus consists in demonstrating that act which makes freedom and necessity two aspects of the same matter: 'Freedom' in Fichte does not mean arbitrariness. It is 'intelligence, which acts and in that sphere the "laws of necessity" obtain[9], – indeed, the core of intelligence *is* the order which thought and rational speech exhibit and which is the condition for the fact that individuals with different ideas and attitudes can communicate at all. And as such it must be the bridge-builder between subjects.

This must mean that Fichte's position is not undermined by Habermas' criticism: The Fichtean subject is not 'solitary, 'trans-mundane' or whatever categorical views Habermas ascribes to the philosopher of subjectivity. If one can call Fichte's reason 'subject-centred' at all, this could only mean that reason *appears* in the shape of the subject; that the individual hereby raises above its natural animal existence and becomes a being that is capable of more than just satisfying its basic needs, struggling for survival and reproducing itself. Deciding to practise reason the individual as subject can also apply the expression 'I' to itself. That is: by virtue of reason the individual constitutes itself as a subject, and being a subject it then exists in the universal.

Thus the philosophical claim of a universal reason seems to end in metaphysics – as in the tradition of philosophy of consciousness but partly also in the sense of the antique metaphysics. What Plato presupposes throughout his dialogues is that there is something which is the true, the good and the just in itself. However, perhaps we should be cautious of hypostatising these ideas in nouns and instead restrict ourselves to transforming them into adjectives for the purpose of expressing judgements about matters of fact and moral acts. But even in this weakened form such judgements inevitably have metaphysical implications, namely insofar as the rational presents itself as an idea of harmony (i.e. 'symmetry', 'equality', 'mutual recognition') which has the *power* to shape the relationships among the participants in a community.

The reality of this power is deeply rooted in the general human attitude that conviction should be preferred to persuasion. Insight is a power because it raises the truth-seeker against the lower power of manipulating rhetoric. Since a power can only be superseded by another power, insight itself – as it is actually able to change the opinion of the individual person – must be such a power, i.e. an idea in action.

In that respect the transcendental idealism of Fichte probably does not differ all that much from the ontology of Plato. Fichte just points out that conviction is the result of a thought which the individual himself decides to produce. It only appears – if at all – if the individual is capable of liberating himself from untried, passively assumed attitudes in nice rhetoric wrappings and he insists on producing the view himself. (Hence Fichte's rejection of every form of dogmatism). Who is not familiar with the situation in which one is inundated with enthusiastic words by somebody who wants to win one over to his point of view. If one gives in passively to escape the flow of words, one is persuaded. But if one follows the principle of not representing an attitude without a sufficient number of good reasons, one expresses something like: "Wait a minute, I must think about what you say." In that case, one insists on acquiring the point actively in order to try it out, in order to produce it oneself, before one answers in the affirmative.

And this legitimates Fichte's view in relation to communicative reason: Even if we must admit that the testing of the validity of norms and statements is a discursive procedure according to certain rules, the rational – the right and the true – result presupposes the subject in the Fichtean sense. Not only the process of seeking the truth but also the rational result must depend on conviction, i.e. it presupposes the active acquisition and trial of the views and arguments that swirl in the air. And as regards Habermas' fear of the solitary, isolated individual the concession to the notion of the subject does not necessarily weaken the integrity of the group; on the contrary, the independently produced point of view alone can express reason and consequently possess universal validity. And do we not rather prefer to be members of a community of masterful men than of a bunch of dependent persons?

## IV. Communication as the means of reason

The essential aim of the dismissal of metaphysics which the shift of paradigm should approach is the sharpening of the sense of the life world, of the finitude of existence. One of Habermas' typical wordings in his attempt to construe post-metaphysical motives of thought sounds as follows: "Das transzendentale Bewusstsein soll sich in der Praxis der Lebenswelt konkretisieren, soll in historischen Verkörperungen Fleisch und Blut gewinnen"[10]. But what do these words cover? That life is finite; that the rational forms of life are historical formations and therefore temporary, no one will deny. But still reason is indispensable for every life that deserves the epithet human. Claiming this point of view, Habermas is traditional and rejects in the name of humanism all sorts of criticism from the quarters of post-modernism, relativism and subjectivism. It could also characterise his own view on every finite historical phenomenon what the young Hegel says about the interesting individuality "…in welcher die Vernunft aus dem Bauzeug eines besonderen Zeitalters sich eine Gestalt organisiert hat"[11]. So even in the age of historical consciousness we cannot escape a philosophy of reason with metaphysical implications. In that matter Habermas is closer to German Idealism than he is willing to acknowledge. Reason and universality are as much at work here as they are there.

Perhaps it is more fruitful to consider Habermas' communicative concept of reason a contribution to rather than an dismissal of the tradition of metaphysics: it could then be the task of the communicative 'turn' in Habermas to teach the already rationally thinking human being a social behaviour and put forward ideals for a healthy, democratic culture of discussion; yes, it might just give the rational consciousness flesh and blood, not reduce it to a social construction.

## Notes

1. Habermas, Jürgen (1992) *Nachmetaphysisches Denken* (Frankfurt am Main, Suhrkamp Verlag) 11ff.
2. Habermas, Jürgen (1988) *Der philosophische Diskurs der Moderne.* (Frankfurt am Main, Suhrkamp Verlag) 54.
3. Habermas, Jürgen (1981) *Theorie des kommunikativen Handelns.* (Frankfurt am Main, Suhrkamp Verlag) vol. 1. 387.
4. (1981) 28.
5. For instance in: Habermas, Jürgen (1983) Diskursethik – Notizen zu einem Begründungsprogram", *Moralbewusstsein und kommunikatives Handeln.* (Frankfurt am Main, Suhrkamp Verlag).
6. The aspects of metaphysical thought which Habermas criticises he sketches out in (1992) *Nachmetaphysisches Denken.* (Frankfurt am Main, Suhrkamp Verlag) 36ff.
7. Fichte, Johann Gottlieb (1984) *Versuch einer neuen Darstellung der Wissenschaftslehre (1797/98)* (Hamburg, Felix Meiner Verlag) 28.
8. (1984) 23.
9. (1984) 24.
10. (1992) 15.
11. Hegel, Georg Wilhelm Friedrich (1970) *Werke 1-20* (Frankfurt am Main, Suhrkamp Verlag) vol. 1. 19.